Love and family light up the darkness.

"Wisdom That Transforms. Action That Lasts."

Our Commitment

We believe that true wisdom has the power to transform lives. Our mission is to equip readers with timeless insights and practical tools that inspire growth, guide decisions, and empower purposeful living. We don't just inform—we empower.

Our books combine profound understanding with real-life application, enabling readers to unlock their potential and navigate life's challenges with clarity and confidence. With each step guided by wisdom, we help you create lasting change and live the life you deserve.

When wisdom meets purpose, transformation follows.

Love and family light up the darkness.

Copyright

CHOOSE Love and Family: Build Strong Relationships, by J. S. Wellman, published by Extra-mile Publishing, Box 465, Thompsons Station, TN 37179,

ISBN 978-1-952359-53-8 (paperback)
ISBN 978-1-952359-54-5 (ebook)

This book is available as an audiobook on our Amazon Life Planning book series page:	

"Practical Wisdom for Real-Life Challenges!

For More Information
About the Life Planning Series:

www.lifeplanningtools.com

Love and family light up the darkness.

Life Planning Series
by J. S. Wellman

CHOOSE Love and Family

Build Strong Relationships

J. S. Wellman

Extra-mile Publishing

This book is available as an audiobook on our Amazon Life Planning book series page:	

Table of Contents

Free PDF
Living Wisely
The Life Planning Guide

A Quick-Start Guide to Purposeful Living and Wise Decisions!

Discover the five life domains: purpose, people, principles, productivity, and perspective. Wisdom is the ability to apply truth and logic to real-life decisions and produce good outcomes. It influences your choices and will produce action that lasts. Consider and apply the five practical wisdom principles for daily living. (6 pages)

Free PDF: https://getwisdompublishing.com/resource-registration/

Free PDF

Five Practical Principles For Life

When wisdom meets purpose, transformation follows.

Free PDF

Wise Decision-Making

[Get the ebook version for 99 cents]

You can make good choices.

This free resource provides a project-oriented perspective and gives ten detailed steps to analyze issues/problems to determine a solution. (26 pages)

Good decisions expand your horizons. Don't allow the fear of decision-making paralyze your ability to make good choices. Think through the reasonable alternatives and move forward. When your eyes are on the goal, making good decisions is easier.

Free PDF: https://getwisdompublishing.com/resource-registration/

Kindle ebook for 99 cents: https://www.amazon.com/dp/B09SYGWRVL/

Ebook

Free PDF

Make Thoughtful Decisions!

Good decisions expand your horizons.

Message From the Author

Unlock Your Potential with Timeless Wisdom!

The general purpose of this book and the Life Planning Series is to encourage you to pursue actions and character traits that will produce your best life. The Series addresses ten different activities or traits that help people improve their lives, and *CHOOSE Core Values* addresses sixteen separate core values that you might consider beneficial.

Understand that you can improve or acquire high personal character and outstanding habits, no matter how good or bad your life may be at the moment. Good personal character and life habits can be achieved.

You don't have to read all the books in this series to make a significant change or improvement in your life. Find the books that focus on the areas of your life that you want to improve and dig in.

Know that this is a progressive journey. You don't need to climb the highest mountain immediately. You may just want to learn more about the basic principles and concepts. This Series and this book will provide you with a foundation for decisions relative to your lifestyle, goals, priorities, and commitments.

The key to developing high character and making good decisions in your life is *intentionality*. The Life Planning Series will help you identify the path you want to travel but you will need to be intentional about walking that path. If you want to make progress toward the goal of living a better life, you must intentionally take action.

Change will require making good decisions, establishing important core values in your life, setting priorities, and making commitments. This book will help you identify the values in life that will produce your goals and objectives. High personal character and good habits can be achieved if you want them.

This Series is designed to help you smooth out the path for your life journey. But, remember, all actions (both words and deeds) have consequences. These consequences will impact you and all those around you.

The key to your success is: "*Decide you want to do it and work at it regularly.*"

Steve

"Set your mind on your future and commit to being the very best you can be!"
Stephen H Berkey[2]

"Wisdom to decide and the steps to succeed."

The Life Planning Series provides real-life tools for wise decision-making and personal transformation

Wisdom to Decide.
Steps to Succeed.
Life Starts Here!

Introduction

Life Planning Based on Wisdom!
Build Wisdom. Build Life!

We want to inform, encourage, and inspire you to choose character and improve your life.

The second and equally important purpose is to help you implement specific changes in your life.

Our third goal is to encourage you to pass it on. It is our desire that you will not only obtain this knowledge, but pass it on to others – particularly friends, children, grandchildren, or students.

An African proverb says, *"Don't spend all day rejoicing on your bench. When you pray, move your feet!"* The message of this proverb is that if you want to accomplish something, nothing will happen if you're sitting on your bench all day.

Growth and improvement, including living a better life, requires action and intentionality. The good news is that you can use the information in this book to acquire knowledge that will help you follow a path to a better life.

Those who want to develop a *total life plan* can do that by acquiring our *Life Planning Handbook*. We will discuss that book later in this chapter.

WHY READ THIS BOOK

The ideal reader of this book is someone who wants to accomplish any of the following:

- learn more about this subject,
- improve your life circumstances,
- live a better life with less stress,
- dig more deeply into the meaning of this subject and how it might impact your life,
- overcome the chaos of life, family or work relationships, or
- learn how to make good or better decisions.

PERSONAL GROWTH

We encourage you to make good choices and improve your personal and family life. This process is often referred to as personal growth or personal development. There are many good reasons for pursuing personal growth in your life:

- to find personal peace, meaning, and purpose,
- to gain more control over life situations,
- to acquire certain skills or abilities,
- to become more disciplined,
- to improve or overcome negative attitudes,
- to expand your horizons,
- to make better decisions,
- to open new avenues of understanding, or
- to change certain outcomes in your life.

It is our hope that this book will help you identify conditions in your life you would like to improve. You may need only some help focusing on the right things. You may just want guidance in finding things you can tweak to make a few changes in your lifestyle. You may want a clearer vision of your goals. Or you may want to do some serious work on some particular aspect of your life. Our Life Planning Series will help you achieve any of these goals and desires.

About *CHOOSE Love & Family*

This book will help you build the relationships that matter most—with love that lasts.

Love and family are two of life's greatest gifts—and often, life's greatest challenges. Whether you're trying to become a better parent, strengthen your marriage, or simply show up more intentionally for the people who matter most, *Choose Love & Family* gives you the tools, wisdom, and clarity to build relationships that truly thrive.

This book is for anyone who:

- wants to understand the meaning and power of real love
- is raising children and needs guidance on parenting and discipline
- feels overwhelmed by relational tension and is searching for peace
- desires to improve their role as a spouse, parent, sibling, or family member
- seeks to make better decisions in the name of love, unity, and growth

Inside, you'll explore:

- The core elements of healthy, lasting love.
- Parenting approaches that combine structure and grace.

- How to communicate love in ways that others feel and receive.
- Strategies for building a strong family foundation rooted in values.
- The importance of intentional decisions in shaping family dynamics.

Whether you're starting a family, healing a strained relationship, or simply want to be more loving and present in your daily life, *Choose Love & Family* offers timeless, practical guidance that can transform your home—and your heart.

THE LIFE PLANNING SERIES

The Life Planning Series covers most of the important subjects that you would address in an attempt to live a good or better life. Most of the books address one particular subject, help you identify your life goals, and guide you in creating action plans to achieve those goals. One exception is the Life Planning Handbook which will help you develop a complete life plan.

The Series in total addresses such topics as integrity, choosing friends, guarding your speech, working with diligence, making sound financial decisions, having a positive self- image, leadership, faith, choosing core values, and love and family.

Transform Your thinking.
Transform Your Life!

Love and family light up the darkness.

THE BOOKS

Go to the Life Planning Series page
to choose the book you want:
https://www.amazon.com/dp/B09TH9SYC4

THE LIFE PLANNING HANDBOOK

This is a unique book in the Life Planning Series. The purpose is to produce a total and complete *Life Plan* for your life. The sections include:

1. Life Principles and Character Attributes
2. Habits
3. Friends and Family Relationships
4. Work and Work Ethic
5. Education

6. Community Service
7. Money and Wealth
8. Health
9. Spiritual

The planning process in the Handbook will examine your skills and abilities, your personal life values, priorities, and commitments. The book will help you identify your life goals and create action steps to achieve those goals.

This book will generate purpose, direction, and growth in your life.

Go to https://www.amazon.com/dp/1952359325 to get your copy now.

Decision Fatigue Ends Here!

A structured approach to turn wisdom into results.

PART I - LOVE

Chapter 1
What is Love?

"Where there is love there is life."
Mahatma Gandhi

GENERAL

What exactly is love? Some of you may remember the line from the movie *Love Story* that suggested "Love means never having to say you're sorry." Although that was a catchy little phrase, it doesn't adequately define love. What does "love" mean to you? With respect to the meaning of love, which of the following descriptions from the "love chapter" in the Bible resonate with you when you think of love?

Love is *patient.*
Love is *kind.*
Love does *not envy.*
Love does *not boast.*
Love is *not proud.*
Love is *not rude.*
Love is *not self-seeking.*
Love is *not easily angered.*
Love keeps *no record of wrongs.*
Love *delights in truth,* not in evil.
Love *always protects.*
Love *always trusts.*
Love *always hopes.*
Love always *perseveres.*
Love *never fails.*

This familiar passage from 1 Corinthians 13 is often read at weddings as brides and grooms gaze adoringly at one another. It would probably be more helpful to their marriage if they framed the words, hung them on the kitchen wall, and read them together each day to remind themselves what love is and how lovers act toward one another. It would also be helpful if parents read and discussed them with their children at the dinner table periodically. Just imagine how *all* relationships would be enhanced if we made these definitions a reality in our lives!

"Love is not just something.
Love is everything."
Rumi

WHAT IS LOVE?

There are many types of love. The English language uses one word for love while other languages use four to six depending on the nature of the relationship that is being described. In this book we are not discussing romantic or brotherly love but something called *agape* love. This type of love means to have "esteem" or "high regard" for someone. Agape love is a type of love that is humble, selfless, and unconditional. It gives even if nothing is received in turn. It puts another's wants and needs above one's own needs. This is also a characteristic of true humility. Agape love will undergo hardship, sacrifice, or suffering for another's benefit. Thus, this type of love is a decision, not an emotion or feeling.

At the other end of the relationship spectrum is "hate." Hate is a very strong feeling of dislike, intense hostility, or even aversion to someone or something. It might be described by the synonyms disgust, loathe, detest, or abhor. It's an intense dislike.[1]

Love and hate are extreme opposites. Hate is often thrown around loosely to mean dislike. You might be surprised to learn that God hates. The Bible says that God hates haughty eyes, a lying tongue, hands that shed blood, hearts that devise wicked schemes, feet that are quick to rush into evil, liars, and people who stir up conflict (Proverbs 6:16-19). Obviously these are not the only things that God hates because He hates all evil. But it is worth noting the specific acts the Bible says God hates, which includes pride, lying, and people who stir up dissention.

Why would God hate a liar? Lying conceals hatred and evil. It can rear its ugly head in various ways: slander, gossip, deceit, and deception. The underlying problem is that the lying and deceit is coming from a hateful heart. Liars are often schemers looking to gain an advantage through hiding or falsifying the truth. Untruthfulness and dishonesty will always destroy a relationship.

One might jump to the conclusion that a "good" person should not hate anything, that hate itself is something to abhor. No, even God hates, so that would not seem to be the logical conclusion. We should hate evil, arrogant pride, evil acts, and perverse conduct. Why? Our human nature left to its own devices will tend to tolerate evil and wickedness. We often avoid or ignore evil because that is the easy or convenient response. We can get so used to the occurrence of evil that we become numb to its existence and impact. That's a dangerous situation. Dishonesty of any kind should disgust us.

"To love and be loved is to feel the sun from both sides."

David Viscott

1 CORINTHIANS 13 LOVE

Let's return to the fifteen phrases from the "love chapter" that describe love and add additional descriptive content that will help us understand the meaning and implications of each term.

> **NOTE:** ***Whether or not you believe in or use the Bible, the "love chapter" provides a universal frame of reference regarding the definition and nature of love.***

is patient: is enduring, tolerant, uncomplaining, long-suffering, or calm
is kind: is caring, thoughtful, helpful, good, considerate, concerned
does not envy: is not jealous, holds no resentment
does not boast: does not brag, show off, or act like a know-it-all
is not proud: is not arrogant, conceited, pompous, or big-headed
is not rude: is courteous, mannered, polite, respectful; or boorish or vulgar
is not self-seeking: is humble; not selfish, self-absorbed, or egotistical
is not easily angered: is self-controlled, composed, peaceable, calm
does not record wrongs: is forgiving, tolerant, and magnanimous
does not delight in evil: dislikes evil; does not take pleasure in evil
rejoices in the truth: honest, keeps promises, high integrity, trustworthy
protects: defends, guards, shields, cares for, watches over
trusts: has faith in, has hope in, believes in, depends upon
hopes: has faith; does not despair, is not despondent
perseveres: persists, keeps at it, sticks with it, carries on, does not quit

What would you conclude about the meaning of *agape* love from these additional descriptions? One obvious conclusion is that the sum of the terms and additional descriptions are extensive. This should not be too surprising since the Bible has a great deal to say about love and how we are to express love to others. The Bible says God is love and strongly directs a follower to love one another. The focus of Biblical love is outward toward others and not about self.

The first time I read through the list of terms describing love with a serious intent to comprehend the totality of the meaning, I was overwhelmed! If you don't feel that way you need to read though the list again. You might want to think about which <u>one</u> of these characteristics of love would be the easiest or hardest for you to practice. Then, consider what it means to practice them all.

How you think about, demonstrate, or ignore these characteristics of love will depend on your particular personality and temperament. If you have to choose one characteristic that is difficult, "*not keeping a record of wrongs,*" would be a good choice. We all say we forgive, but we don't forget. "*Not delighting in evil*" might be the easiest one for most people to practice.

It's important to recognize that this list of fifteen characteristics is not an all-inclusive list defining love. It certainly covers much of the subject but the Biblical text does not say or imply that this is a complete description of this very complex subject. In my opinion there are several obvious concepts missing: grace, compassion, and justice. Grace may be the essence of love, compassion is love in action, and justice would require no favoritism and being accountable.

"The greatest thing you'll ever learn is
just to love and be loved in return."
Nat King Cole

Love is patient

Patience in agape love is often the ability to endure difficult or frustrating situations with a calm and understanding attitude. It is being able to wait for calm to return before trying to resolve a problem. It is not motivated by a need to react immediately. For example, patience would take time to listen in times of stress. It requires one to be gentle with others when they are in the middle of chaos. Patience allows one to take time to consider and evaluate when faced with a problem or a mistake. It may mean allowing a relationship to advance slowly and grow more naturally.

Relationships often take time and effort to cultivate and grow. Trying to rush a relationship is not necessarily the best course of action. There will be times when you disagree with your friends or when they make you angry. When we are patient with each other, we create a safe environment in which we can communicate our feelings and needs without fear of judgment or retaliation. This allows us to resolve conflict peacefully and naturally in an appropriate timeframe.

Patience demonstrates love to others. When we are patient with someone, we show them that we care about them and that we are willing to wait for their time-frame. It demonstrates our willingness to wait until they have mentally or emotional reached the point at which they can make a decision or take some action. Patience provides a sense of security and acceptance in a relationship.

Imagine that you are baking a cake. Agape love waits for the cake to bake, even though it is taking a long time. Agape love would not be opening the oven door repeatedly to check on the status of the cake. Other types of love, such as romantic love or parental love, often tend to be more conditional. We might be more likely to wait patiently for a cake to bake if it is our favorite or if it is for a special occasion or purpose. But agape love is selfless and unconditional. It's about being patient with the process and allowing things to develop naturally, even if it takes more time than you may desire.

"Love is an endless act of forgiveness.
Forgiveness is the key
to action and freedom."

Maya Angelou

Love is kind

Kindness in agape love is the act of being considerate or helpful to others without seeking anything in return. It is selfless and motivated by a genuine concern for the well-being of another. For example, a kind person might help a neighbor with grocery shopping or mowing a yard. But kindness can also be demonstrated by simple politeness, like opening a door for someone, saying "thank you," or giving someone a compliment. It can be simply listening to someone pour out their heart about the tough times they are experiencing.

Kindness is an important part of agape love because it is a real physical act of love. When we are kind to others, we are showing them that we care about them and that we want to make their lives better in some way. They hold some level of priority in our lives.

Kindness helps build trust and create a sense of community in which people in a group receive love from others in that community. Kindness often results because someone is conscious of the need of another and is aware of opportunities to help.

Kindness can be demonstrated through forgiveness, particularly if the circumstances are somewhat trying. Kind people give second chances. Kind people tend to be humble and caring about both the needs and wants of others. Being kind is a choice, just like agape love is a choice. Anyone can choose to be kind. It doesn't require special skill. You only need a desire to help someone or simply want to make the world a better place. Love and kindness can melt even the strongest hearts.

***"Love and kindness are never wasted.
They always make a difference.
They bless the one who receives them,
and they bless you, the giver."***
Barbara De Angelis

Love does not envy

Not being envious is the ability to rejoice in the success and happiness of others without feeling jealous or resentful. It is a selfless form of love that is not motivated by a desire to compete or to be better than others.
Not being envious is being happy for a friend when they get a promotion. It's being supportive of a friend's new relationship. It means being happy when a friend's child wins a sporting event over your child's team. It is applauding the success of a colleague or competitor.

If we are not envious of others, we are more likely to be supportive and encouraging. We are also more likely to be honest and open in our communication, allowing for a safe and supportive environment in which people feel they can be themselves.

Here are several tips for practicing not being envious:

- Focus on your own blessings.
- Be grateful for what you have.
- Don't compare yourself or your family to others.
- Celebrate the success of others.
- Don't regard life as a competition.
- Be encouraging to others.

Not being envious is often a process. It may take time and effort to rejoice in the success of others without feeling resentful. But that's what love requires. Ego is a strong influence on our emotions and must be held in check so that envy does not negatively influence our behavior.

Love doesn't envy, and it doesn't boast.
It isn't proud. It never gives up,
and it never stops giving.

Love is being humble, not proud

Humility in agape love is the ability to see yourself accurately and to put other's needs ahead of your own. It is a selfless form of love that is not motivated by a desire for attention or praise. It is the ability not to elevate oneself. Thus, one might do the dishes without being asked or not seek attention or praise for some kindness performed. Admitting mistakes and being honest about shortcomings are also characteristics of being humble. If you tend to be proud you will hesitate to ask for help when it is needed.

Humility means you will admit when you are wrong and take responsibility for the consequences of your actions. In agape love humility creates an environment of equality and respect. Thus, we are more likely to see others as our equals and to treat them with dignity. We are also more likely to be open to receiving help and support from others. This creates stronger and more supportive relationships.

Humility creates an environment of openness and trust. When we are humble, we are more likely to be honest and transparent with others. We will also be more open to feedback and willing to change our behavior.

Several tips for practicing humility include:

- Being willing to learn and take instruction or correction from others.
- Being open to feedback and criticism.
- Serving others without expecting something in return.
- Giving others credit for their accomplishments, particularly when you are part of the team that achieved the result.
- Asking for help when you need it.

There will be times when we fail to be humble, ignoring the needs of others. When that happens we must force ourselves to correct our behavior and fix the situation. When we make a conscious effort to be humble, we strengthen relationships and elevate the important people in our lives.

Imagine that you are in a band. Agape love in the form of humility puts the success of the band before your own personal success. You would be willing to play a less glamorous role in the band, if it meant that the band would be more successful.

Or, imagine that you are coaching a child's soccer team. Humility would drive you to coach the team because you want to help children learn and grow. Your coaching would not be performed because your child is on the team and you want to be sure they get to play.

The Bible speaks of the result of being humble in a very unique way. It says that the first shall be last and the last shall be first. This description not only helps us understand the nature of humility, but it contains a clear warning against pride.

"Humble people don't think less of themselves;
they just think of themselves less.
Love is thinking of others
before thinking of yourself."

Rick Warren

Love is being courteous and polite, not rude

Being *courteous and polite* means you act respectful and are considerate of others, even when it is difficult. Love is not rude, crude, or insensitive. It is a caring way of interacting with others, regardless of their social status, background, or beliefs.

You may allow someone to go ahead of you in line or offer to carry their packages. Polite people listen and do not interrupt. They certainly do not use coarse language. They will say "please" and "thank you." They will open the door for you.

Being courteous and polite is desirable because it creates an environment of trust and stability. When we are polite, we are inherently giving respect to others, indicating we value them and their well-being. Courteous people are conscious of their words and how they will be received or interpreted. Polite people often put themselves in the shoes of another before they speak or act.

We should desire to be polite to others in the hope that we are not treated rudely in return. Be grateful for the people in your life and show them appreciation whenever possible because they will return the favor. Courtesy is not about being perfect. Everyone makes mistakes. But when we make a conscious effort to be polite to others, we are showing them that we care about them and that we value the relationship. That effort will often cause them to be polite to you, even when that might not be their normal behavior or reaction.

If you are in a serious relationship, agape love would insist you treat others as you would want to be treated. You would never be insulting and you would demonstrate care and compassion toward that other person. You would do this even when the other person failed or treated you badly. Agape love is *unconditional*. You chose to treat another with respect and honor at all times, not just when they "earn" it.

"Kindness and politeness are not overrated at all. They're underused."

Tommy Lee Jones

Love is being self-controlled and not easily angered

Self-control in agape love is the ability to manage one's emotions and resulting behaviors in order to act in a loving and caring way, even when such a response may not be warranted. You respond with grace rather than with insult, revenge, or some other form of retaliation. You do not say something hurtful even if you are hurt or angry. You forgive someone who hurts you, even when it is difficult.

You learn to say no to things that would be hurtful in a relationship. The needs of others are important to you and self-control enables you to speak with dignity and respect. You are not mean, aggressive, or out of control.

Self-control is important because it allows us to sustain and build long-term relationships. When we control our emotions and behaviors, we are less likely to say or do things that could hurt others. It is much easier to resolve difficulties peacefully and quickly if we are under control and not saying hurtful or unwarranted things.

Here are some tips for developing self-control:

- Take a deep breath before you speak or act if you think you are under stress.
- Always think in advance about the consequences of what you are doing or saying.
- Think about your motives. Why, exactly, are you doing or saying this?
- Don't let anger, jealousy, or revenge determine what you do or say.
- If your emotions are driving your behavior, take a break and find something else to do.
- Don’t shout or speak harshly to your friends and loved ones.

When you make a conscious effort to develop self-control, you will strengthen your relationships and be able to have very special and close friends that last a lifetime. When you are angry, aggressive, rude, uncaring, or distant, it will be impossible to maintain good or meaningful relationships for any length of time.

"Patience and self-control are the most important skills you can develop. They enable you to sustain and enhance love."

Jack Kornfield

Love does not keep track of wrongs; it forgives

Forgiveness in an agape love context is the act of letting go of hurt or resentment towards someone who has hurt you. Love forgives. It means that you forgive a partner or friend who makes a mistake, even a serious one, because you choose to love them. You forgive a child who does something wrong simply because you choose to, even though the mistake may have been costly. You may even forgive a betrayal or broken heart, because that is what love does.

Forgiveness allows you to heal and move on from hurt. It is not pleasant or desirable to live in or extend a season of hurt. The sooner it is resolved the better.

When you forgive someone, you are not saying that what they did was acceptable. You are simply releasing yourself from the burden of carrying around the baggage of anger and resentment. This allows you to focus on the present while moving forward with your life. If you stay bogged down in anger, life will be difficult.

When you forgive, you create a new and often stronger relationship. It is very important to acknowledge your pain in order to allow yourself to grieve the hurt or loss. Focus on the present and the future, rather than dwelling on the past. Remember, forgiveness is about you, not about them. But you may have to set boundaries to protect yourself from being hurt again until you know the situation has been corrected or resolved.

Forgiveness is not always easy, but it is necessary to move your life forward and to continue to love. Suppose you are in a car accident. The other driver is at fault, but they are also injured. Agape love would help the other driver even though they caused the accident. Agape love would put the needs of the other driver equal to your own, even though you are also hurt and angry. Does this sound impossible? It may be! Depending on the nature of the situation, a lot of time may be necessary to get past the hurt. But it's required for love. Forgiving and letting go of past wrongs is crucial for love that builds toward a better future.

"Forgiveness does not change the past,
but it does enlarge the future."
Paul Boese

Love is honest, truthful, and trustworthy

Being *honest and trustworthy* means you are truthful, reliable, and dependable. It is a selfless form of love that is not motivated by a desire to deceive or manipulate others. You tell the truth!

Truth does not mean you tell others what they want to hear. Truth is generally the best option, even if it is inconvenient, scary, or potentially hurtful. Never lie about your feelings and emotions. You can do little to prevent them and you must manage your life around them. Feelings and emotions are neither true nor false, they just are. You may hate something. That hate may be irrational, but you still hate it. It's like the person who is freaked out by a little harmless garden snake. No matter how illogical that may be, they are still truly frightened.

Being truthful means you keep promises in all circumstances. It means admitting your mistakes, errors, and wrong-doing. Your honesty will help you develop a reputation for reliability and dependability. You cannot be in a relationship and be untrustworthy!

When we are honest and trustworthy with others, we allow others to be vulnerable and honest with us. This helps to build deep and meaningful connections. Being trustworthy is also necessary in resolving conflicts effectively. When we are honest with each other about our feelings, we are more likely to be able to find solutions that work for everyone involved. Loving relationships built on trust are strong and far more resilient.

Agape love can be illustrated by the example of building a house using the highest quality materials and construction methods. The best result will be attained if it is done right, even if it is more expensive and time-consuming. You want the house to be strong and durable, as if you were going to live in it the rest of your life.

"Integrity is doing the right thing, even when no one is watching."
C.S. Lewis

Love perseveres; it never gives up

Perseverance is the ability to stick with something, even when it is difficult. It is a form of love that refuses to quit. It means that you stay in a relationship even when it is challenging. Thus, you may continue a relationship even if you have been hurt. It may mean that you care for a loved one who is sick or disabled. You may need to support them through challenging times in their career. You never give up on them, even if they give up on themselves.

When we persevere through the difficult times, our relationships become stronger, more resilient, and ultimately more meaningful. When we persevere in loving someone, we are showing them that we are committed to them, no matter what.

Persevering is not always easy, but it is worth it if you truly love the other person. You cannot have a long-term relationship without perseverance. It's like when you plant a tree. Agape love would water and fertilize the tree, even when it is small and fragile. It would tend to the tree, even when it is not producing much fruit. After the tree is grown it needs to be trimmed and sometimes even pruned. All of these acts are directed at helping the tree thrive. This also applies to loving relationships.

"It does not matter how slowly you go as long as you do not stop."
Confucius

This brings us to the last three characteristics that I suggested were missing from the 1 Corinthians 13 list: grace, compassion, and justice. We will briefly discuss those next.

Love provides grace and pardon. It does not devalue

*Grace i*s the act of providing favor, approval, or mercy to someone even though they may not deserve it. It is giving kindness instead of punishment. It is a reprieve, do-over, or "mulligan" in the game of golf. Someone makes a mistake and out of love you do not respond or retaliate in kind. In effect you, you forgive.

Love, in the context of grace, is characterized by the ability to forgive and overlook the faults and mistakes of others. It may mean being understanding, kind, or compassionate, when faced with the hurts caused by others.

Pardon, on the other hand, is much like forgiveness. It requires letting go of resentment and grievances. These attributes contribute to creating a supportive and accepting environment in which individuals and families can grow and thrive despite their flaws.

To love someone with grace means we accept them as they are and avoid judging or condemning them for their weaknesses or mistakes. It means we forgive them when they hurt us, and seek forgiveness when we hurt them.

Loving others with grace is not necessarily easy or cheap. It may require our sacrifice, humility, and courage. It could challenge us to overcome our own selfishness, pride, and fear. One might suggest that love with grace or pardon is the highest form of love, and the most rewarding.

Love is compassionate. It is sympathetic and warmhearted

Love is *compassionate* and is characterized by a deep and genuine concern for the well-being of another. Compassion involves a profound understanding of someone else's struggles and a desire to alleviate their problems and suffering.

Being sympathetic means showing empathy and understanding towards another's situation and experiences. It produces acts of generosity and benevolence. A warmhearted, loving person will express love and caring with tenderness and affection. Love encompassing these attributes creates a nurturing and supportive relationship that promotes both physical and emotional well-being and happiness.

Agape love is a powerful decision. It demonstrates kindness, understanding, and care for others, especially those to whom we are emotionally attached like family and close friends.

To love someone with compassion, sympathy, and warm-heartedness means to empathize with their feelings and experiences, and share in their joys and sorrows. It means we feel sorry for them when they are hurt or troubled and we offer comfort and support.

Loving with compassion and warmheartedness is not selfish or demanding. It does not expect anything in return, but rather gives freely and unconditionally. It does not judge or criticize, but rather accepts and appreciates. It does not hold grudges or resentments, but rather forgives and heals. It does not fear or avoid, but rather embraces and cherishes.

Love is being just and impartial

Lastly, love means we *treat others fairly* and without bias. In this context, love is not influenced by favoritism or discrimination. It implies that decisions and actions are guided by a sense of justice, ensuring that others are treated with equal consideration and respect.

Impartiality in love means avoiding unfair preferences, decisions, or actions. Being impartial means we are objective and unbiased. Love marked by justice contributes to a healthy and balanced relationship in which each individual feels valued and respected.

These qualities show fairness, equality, and respect for others, especially those who are related or close to us. We would treat those we love according to the same standards and principles that we apply to ourselves. It means we recognize their rights and treat them with dignity. We listen to their opinions and value their contribution. At times it may require that we recognize their faults and correct them with kindness and honesty.

Loving others with justice and impartiality is not blind or indifferent. It does not ignore or tolerate wrongdoing, but rather seeks to reconcile. It does not favor or exclude, but rather attempts to include and embrace the positive and good things in life. It is a noble and often challenging form of love that we should seek for all our relationships.

THE MOST IMPORTANT CHARACTERISTICS

How might we summarize these characteristics of love? In my opinion, the three most important characteristics are honesty, humility, and forgiveness. Why these three?

Honesty is the bedrock of personal character. If you do not act with honesty and integrity, live your life based on truth, and be worthy of trust, then you are nothing. I might even say worthless.

Humility is the characteristic that is almost God-like. If you are truly humble you put the needs of others equal to or higher than your own. What more could a friend or spouse desire?

Forgiveness is the characteristic that covers all the failures. If you fail or if others fail in any of the other character traits that make up love, you can continue in the loving relationship because you forgive or are forgiven.
If you want to develop or improve love in your life, focus on these three: honesty, humility, and forgiveness.

Love thrives on honesty and transparency.
Love, like true humility,
doesn't hold grudges or seek revenge.
Love is an endless act of forgiveness,
providing openness and acceptance.

Honesty

Honesty is the foundation of trust. Without honesty, it is impossible to build a real relationship. When we are honest with our partners and friends, we are showing them that we respect and value them. This creates a place for being vulnerable and honest with one another.

Honesty is essential for communication. Communication is fundamental to any successful relationship. When we are honest with others, we are able to communicate our needs and feelings openly. This allows us to resolve conflict and to build a deeper connection with others.

Honesty shows others that we are authentic and sincere. When we are genuine with our friends, we are showing them who we really are. This allows them to know us on a deeper level and love us for who we are. We are sincere and genuine with those we love.

Humility

Humility is necessary for healthy conflict resolution. When we are humble, we are able to admit when we are wrong. This allows us to resolve conflict and build stronger relationships. Everyone makes mistakes. When we are humble, we are able to learn from our mistakes and grow as individuals. This helps build more resilient relationships.

Honesty and humility are both extremely important because they are essential for building trust and intimacy. When we are honest and humble we show others that we respect them and value their trust. This allows us to communicate openly and honestly. It shows our friends that we are authentic and willing to learn, grow, and build lasting relationships.

Forgiveness

Forgiveness is important because it allows us to let go of anger and resentment. When we forgive someone we are not saying we accept what they did; we are simply releasing ourselves from the burden of ongoing anger or resentment. This allows us to heal and move on from current or past hurts.

Summary

Love is the purest form of humility, because we put the needs and desires of others ahead of our own. It requires honesty. We must be transparent with our emotions, fears, and insecurities when we truly love. In the face of imperfections and mistakes, love finds the strength to forgive, understanding that we are all flawed and we all need the compassion of others.

"Love is not possession, love is freedom.
Love is not restriction, love is expansion.
Love is not domination, love is liberation.
Love is not death, love is life."
Leo Buscaglia

Wisdom to Action Challenge

Consider the relationships in your life. Which ones truly enhance your well-being and allow you to express your authentic self? Identify one action you can take this week to deepen these connections and align more closely with your core identity within them.

Chapter 2
Love Cares

"Power at its best is love implementing the demands of justice, and justice at its best is power correcting everything that stands against love."

Martin Luther King Jr.

LOVE YOURSELF FIRST

Society today is very focused on self, the promotion of self, and the celebration of self. This focus suggests that the individual is paramount and has the right to demand recognition if they so desire. It produces the idea that we must love ourselves before we can love others.

The arguments for this concept are similar to airline companies telling us to put on our own oxygen mask first before we help our neighbor or child. Advocates for loving ourselves first would suggest the following:

1. You are unique and special.
2. You should know both your strengths and your weaknesses and act accordingly.
3. You should educate yourself and intentionally improve yourself and circumstances.
4. You should avoid negative, proud, and evil people.
5. You should celebrate your successes.

Loving yourself centers around the idea that you must focus on yourself first before you can love somebody else. This sounds logical and is certainly popular in contemporary thought. But, is it really true? Is it partially true? Or is it false?

I can certainly understand why not liking yourself might create relationship problems. If you are self-absorbed and self-centered, people are not going to want to associate with you. Who wants to spend time with someone who regards himself as a loser or considers himself the smartest guy on the planet?

But do these attitudes determine a person's ability to love others? I'm not so sure. We should all love ourselves to some degree, but the point of this question deals with loving self being the primary and necessary requirement to love others. It implies that you can't love others without first loving yourself.

It is interesting to observe that the Bible, which spends a great amount of time describing love, says very little about loving oneself. The overwhelming focus of the Bible is on loving others, not self. Nothing is ever said about loving yourself. The closest the Bible gets to any statement about loving oneself is the command to love your neighbor "as yourself" (Romans 13:9). But even here the primary focus is on loving our neighbor and the degree to which that love should be shown. The focus is not on self.

Some suggest that if you can't or won't take care of yourself, you can't care for others. But I am not sure that has been adequately proven. Should you take care of yourself? Yes, of course. But having minimal concern for yourself may come from low self-esteem, not the inability or lack of desire to help others.

LOVE IS ACTION

In his book, *"Dad, The Family Coach,"* Dave Simmons tells of an act of love that occurred in a mall. One day he took his eight year old Helen and five-year-old Brandon to the Cloverdale Mall. He wanted to buy some tools at Sears. When they arrived at the parking lot, there was a big sign that said, "Petting Zoo." Immediately the kids asked, "Can we go, Daddy? Can we go? Please." Since it would not be any real trouble, Dave said, "Sure," and handed both his kids a quarter.

A few minutes later he was making his way down the aisle when he spotted Helen slowly walking up behind him. She looked up at him and said, "Well, Daddy, it cost fifty cents. So, I gave Brandon my quarter." Then she said the most beautiful thing of all. She repeated the family motto, "Love is action!"

What do you think he did? Not what you might think. Dave finished his shopping and then took Helen back to the petting zoo. They stood by the fence watching Brandon go crazy petting and feeding the animals. Helen stood with her hands and her chin resting on the fence just watching. Dave felt fifty cents in his pocket, almost burning a hole through the material, but he never offered it, and she never asked for it. Helen was following through with the lessons she had been taught.[2]

Agape love is not just action, but action that requires a sacrifice. Love often has a price: it costs something. It is like Christian salvation, someone paid the price. When you love, benefits accrue to or for someone else. Love is almost always extended outward toward another, it is giving not taking.

The *Power of Love Newspaper* columnist and minister, George Crane told a story about a wife who came into his office full of hatred toward her husband. "I do not only want to get rid of him; I want to get even. Before I divorce him, I want to hurt him as much as he has me." Dr. Crane suggested an ingenious plan. "Go home and act as if you really love your husband. Tell him how much he means to you. Praise him for every decent trait. Go out of your way to be as kind, considerate, and generous as possible. Spare no efforts to please him, to enjoy him. Make him believe you love him. After you've convinced him of your undying love and that you cannot live without him, you can then drop the bomb and tell him you're getting a divorce. That will really hurt him."

With revenge in her eyes, she smiled and exclaimed, "Beautiful, beautiful. Will he ever be surprised!" And she did it with enthusiasm. Acting as she was told. For two months she showed love, kindness, listening, giving, and sharing. Two months passed. She didn't return. Dr. Crane called. "Are you ready now to go through with the divorce?" "Divorce?" she exclaimed. "Never, I discovered I really do love him."

Her actions had not only changed her feelings but his as well. Love really does require action. Her acts of love and kindness resulted in real feelings and emotion. The ability to love is cemented in our hearts by deeds not just words of sweet nothings whispered in someone's ear.[3]

"Life without love
is like a tree without
blossoms or fruit."

Khalil Gibran

LOVE ONE ANOTHER

Agape love is not about what we "feel" or about skin-tingling emotion. True a*gape* love is caring and adoration in action. Some might suggest that the ultimate act of love would be *"that we lay down our life for a friend."* Assuming this extreme response of laying down your life is not ever demanded of you, what kind of normal acts might you engage in that would demonstrate your *agape* love for someone else?

There are many. Since I have chosen to use the Bible as a source for describing the meaning and nature of agape love, allow me to use it as a source for describing how to demonstrate such love for "one another." I put these last two words in quotes because there are fifty some descriptions in the Bible telling us how to treat "one another." Here are about a third of those instructions:

Encourage one another (Hebrews 3:13, 10:24-25)
Build up one another (Romans 14:19; 1 Thessalonians 5:11)
Be kind to one another (1 Thessalonians 5:15)
Live in harmony with one another (Romans 12:16)
Be devoted to one another (Romans 12:10)
Accept one another. (Romans 15:7)
Serve one another. (Galatians 5:13)
Have concern for one another. (1 Corinthians 12:25)
Carry each other's burdens. (Galatians 6:2)
Teach and admonish one another. (Colossians 3:16)
Pray for one another. (James 5:16)
Don't judge one another. (Romans 14:13)
Don't slander one another. (James 4:11)
Don't provoke one another. (Galatians 5:26)
Speak truth to one another (Ephesians 4:25)
Be humble with one another (1 Pet 3:8, 5:5; Phil 2:3)
Forgive one another (Mt 5:24, 6:14-15; Col 3:13b)

"If you judge people,
you have no time
to love them."
Mother Teresa

Honesty, humility, and forgiveness

The above "one another" instructions are generally easy to understand. They do not require much explanation. They do confirm, as I mentioned earlier, the broad and extensive meaning of the nature of agape love. If you remember, we suggested in Chapter 1 that in the fifteen characteristics of love described in 1 Corinthians 13 there were three that were the most important: honesty, humility, and forgiveness.

It is instructive to recognize the consistency of the "one another" statements in the Bible to the definition statements about love in 1 Corinthians 13. These three occur in the "one another" statements and are the last three listed above. This not only demonstrates the consistency of the Bible, but emphasizes the importance of these three characteristics.

Remember what we said earlier about these three attributes:

> *Honesty is the bedrock of personal character. If you do not act with honesty and integrity, live your life based on truth, and be worthy of trust, then you are nothing.*
>
> *Humility is the characteristic that is almost God-like. If you are truly humble you put the needs of others equal to or higher than your own. What more could a friend or spouse desire?*

> *Forgiveness is the characteristic that covers all the failures. If you fail or if others fail in any of the other character traits that make up love, you can continue in a loving relationship because you forgive or are forgiven.*

WE MUST BE FAIR

Does loving one another mean that we must treat each other with fairness? I have to admit that I have an inherent bias against the concept of being fair. Being fair generally means that we treat people in a way that does not favor one over another. That certainly seems like a reasonable concept at first glance. It means equal treatment for all parties. But that does not necessarily produce the best or right result.

Let me state unequivocally, I don't think "being fair" should be one of the elements of love. On too many occasions it can be the wrong decision because treating everyone equally can produce an undesirable result.

It is not always fair to give the same opportunities to individuals with different levels of expertise or need. Some individuals may have more advantages or opportunities to begin with and giving those persons something they really don't need is not beneficial. Or, giving persons that need more help less than they need does not produce the desired result. Fairness should not reinforce disparities.

Some social justice advocates suggest that "true fairness" must address historical and systemic inequalities that exist. This often requires providing additional or different support or opportunities to people who lack certain skills or abilities because they were denied access to education or training that others were given or allowed to pursue.

Fairness is hardly ever the best course of action for disaster relief situations. It is always necessary to prioritize the most needy individuals over those not in a serious situation. Fairness can also create conflict in situations where resources are limited. It may not be beneficial to allocate limited resources equally, but rather where they can do the most good or have the greatest impact.

Equal treatment in a family can also produce undesirable results. Giving more understanding and attention to a child or friends who emotionally need more personal contact can enhance the relationships of all concerned. Different treatment based on need and the well-being of both the group and individuals should be the chosen course of action, even if it's not "fair" in a strictly objective sense.

The argument against always being "fair" is centered on the concept that rigid adherence to fairness can lead to unjust or undesirable results. During the Covid-19 debacle, money was given to many people who did not need it, but to be "fair" many people received money and financial help that was not needed and often totally unwarranted.

Context does matter. There are situations where other values such as equity, efficiency, justice, and even common sense should take precedence over being fair. We should always carefully consider the specific circumstances and goals in each situation to determine the most appropriate course of action.

SUSTAINING LOVING RELATIONSHIPS

Relationships don't exist by themselves! Friends require time and effort. Family is hard work and requires constant time and attention. If you have worked hard at attaining a good relationship, be assured you must work equally hard at maintaining it.

An old saying that is attributed to Teddy Roosevelt is, "People don't care how much you know, until they know how much you care." The secret to love is caring for others. Knowledge is not enough. Compassion and empathy are needed to produce action that results in truly effective love and caring.

It's like the person who expresses concern about another person who is cold because they don't have a coat or can't afford fuel for their heater. What good are such feelings and concerns unless they do something about the need and help alleviate it? There is no value in or credit due the person who sees or identifies a problem and then does nothing to alleviate it.

It is almost always necessary in any kind of circumstances to separate reality from feelings and emotions. If you are a particularly emotional person and tend to wear your emotions on your sleeve, managing your emotions and feelings will be important in order to maintain a normal or reasonable relationship with others. The key to making good decisions is based on facts, not feelings.

If you have a strong self-identity or high self-esteem, it is often much easier to maintain good relationships. If you know your strengths and weaknesses you can avoid doing things where your weaknesses are required and tend to rely on your strengths in order to achieve success at what you are doing. Knowing yourself well and understanding your temperament and personality can be a big advantage in sustaining good relationships.

If you are a compassionate person, that compassion will be attractive to your friends and associates. If you are not strong in this area, try to think about the needs of others and how you can help. Be particularly aware when friends are struggling and not only supply verbal comfort but think about how you might actually be able to help.

Being able to compromise in serious relationships will also be a big advantage. If you are one that tends to always want it done your way, you will struggle to maintain close relationships. Think in terms of "we" rather than "me." Be willing to do things that are new to you in order to accommodate the desires of others. Be willing to go places and do things that are not high on your bucket list. In individual or group relationships everyone must give a little. Don't try to force your friends to do all the giving.

If things go badly, don't blame someone, but rather just laugh it off. We all make mistakes, so when someone else messes up, don't try to make them feel bad. Just remember, the next time it might be your mistake. Life is not about winners and losers but about joy and contentment. Nobody wants to live life on the edge of anxiety and be worrying about making mistakes. Mistakes are a part of life. Fix them and move on.

Frequent and clear communication is important in all relationships. Every Hallmark love story movie has an incident where there is a misunderstanding that could easily have been avoided if the participants had simply asked questions and clarified the situation. Don't make assumptions – it is very easy to misunderstand or misinterpret. You must value honest and open communication in order to maintain good relationships.

In order to sustain relationships, one very necessary attribute is compassion for others. It's important in any relationship to recognize the needs of other people. Most people can be generally encouraging and perform random acts of kindness from time to time. But it is better to be more intentional about showing or demonstrating love toward others than to just let it happen when it bubbles up to the top of your consciousness.

Here are some easy ways to practice love and compassion:

- Send notes of congratulations or encouragement.
- Help someone who is depressed (or "blue" as my grandmother would say).
- Help do things that the other person cannot physically do. Old age comes to all of us.
- Be positive. Do not grumble or whine. Have an attitude that lifts up, not tears down.
- Forgive others and don't demand they forgive you.
- Guard your speech. Speak gentle words of encouragement that bring light, not darkness.
- Be in control of your feeling and emotions. Excessive emotions can be a turn-off.
- Be patient with others. Let them operate in their time, not yours.
- Be humble. Put the needs of others high on your radar. Make others feel important.
- Be generous with your time, skills, and presence.

Lastly, be trustworthy. If you can't trust your friends or your friends cannot trust you, there is no basis for a relationship. Truthfulness is the bedrock of relationships.

"Love is that condition in which the happiness of another person is essential to your own."
Robert A. Heinlein

TEN TIPS FOR LOVING OTHERS

Here are some easy tips for how to love others:

1. ENCOURAGEMENT: Give compliments and credit to others. Pump up your friends when they have done something well or completed some task or achievement.

2. ATTITUDE: Smile at your friends – strangers too. No one wants to look at a grumpy face!

3. LUNCH: Encourage someone who is depressed or going through a tough time in their life. Take them to lunch and get them away from their routine.

4. HELP: Do a favor for a friend, neighbor, or co-worker who needs something to brighten their day. Or just do it because you like them and want to bring them joy.

5. VISIT: Be present when somebody is home-bound or needs somebody to talk to. Read to or visit with people in a nursing home. Visit elderly family members.

6. FOOD DELIVERY: Take a meal or snack to your neighbor, a hurting friend, or a loved one.

7. SOCIAL: Invite neighbors, friends, family, or co-workers to your home for dinner or dessert.

8. BABYSIT: Offer to babysit for your grandchildren, a single mom, or a neighbor.

9. TRANSPORTATION: Give a ride to the elderly to church, doctor, or the store.

If you have hurt or angered someone, shower them with some act of love. Love covers over many offenses. We all do and say dumb things. Don't let a short lapse in judgment ruin a relationship. Ask for forgiveness, if necessary, and accompany the request with a gesture that shows you truly care.

FINAL THOUGHTS

Think about what it means on a real and practical basis to "*love your neighbor as yourself*." My first reaction when seriously thinking about this suggestion was that it is not possible. There is no way we in our human condition could even think about reaching this unique and impossible state. Not only would it be difficult to put somebody in the same category, but then the implication is that I would not expect anything in return for my gracious attitude or help.

You may have heard some parent state that they would give their life for a child. Again, that is not likely to ever be the actual situation, but a parent could certainly wish they could experience the emotional hurt or physical sickness in place of a child.

As you mature you will experience the sadness and disappointment of being let down by someone you admire or love. They should not have been disloyal or dishonest, but they were. You will probably have your heart damaged, broken or shattered, maybe more than once. You may break the hearts of others because love is a combination of facts, feelings, and emotions that penetrate the soul and you failed them.

You may argue or fight with your best friend, spouse, or parent. You may blame new friends for things an old one said or did. You will have great sadness when time passes so fast that you lose someone you really love, and you intended to say you were sorry before they were gone . . .

Put those memories in a safe place, take a lot of photos, and keep loved ones close. Live life to the fullest! Don't let good relationships pass you by or fade. Treat people as though you may never see them again. Kindness is important, goodness is critical, but love conquers all.

"Love is not a being word, it is an action word... When you see hate out there, understand that the challenge will never be the hate of some, but the silence, indifference, and apathy of the many."
Senator Cory Booker

MY ADMISSION

The Truth

As I finish the writing of the first section of this book, I realize how miserably I fail at most of what I just described. As I look back at the three characteristics of honesty, humility, and forgiveness that I said were the three most important characteristics of love, I am faced with the reality that I don't measure up well. I'm relatively honest, I don't rob banks – but don't dig too deeply into my character, please! I fail the greatest at being humble. I have great difficulty with empathy. Yes, I may provide somebody financial support, but don't ask me to get too involved personally.

I suspect most of you reading this book have similar admissions to some extent, but with other aspects of love. At a minimum we all would like to be better than we are and we may struggle with how to make that happen.

The Problem

Unfortunately if you think there is a human solution, I think you are wrong. I don't know of anyone on their own that can truly and fully love. And, many of us can't even improve much. That's the problem!

The Solution

So, what's the solution? Well, that is not a subject for this book. I am totally convinced we can't do it under our own power. If you want to truly love, you will absolutely need a higher power in your life. If that is something that you want to pursue, pick up a copy, of *Choose Faith* in the Life planning series:

https://www.amazon.com/dp/1952359473

"Never struggle to chase love, affection, or attention. If it isn't given freely by another person, it isn't worth having."
Lucille Ball

Wisdom to Action Challenge

Reflect on your daily interactions. How can you intentionally incorporate more acts of caring love into your routine? Identify one specific act of kindness you will perform each day this week and observe the impact it has on your well-being and those around you.

Chapter 3
My Love Plan

In most all of the other books in the Life Planning Series we provided a process to develop a substantial plan and specific action steps for the given character trait that would help you improve your life. If this is your first book in this Series, we recommend picking up *CHOOSE Integrity*, because honesty and integrity are core life principles. That book contains the more extensive planning process that you could adapt for this book if you so wish.

This book will provide an abbreviated approach to the planning process for improving your love or family skills.

1. Love Definition:
Choose one of the following. Circle the trait you want to work on and make notes to the right of what you want to do to make the chosen characteristic real in your life.

Love is *patient.*
Love is *kind.*
Love does *not envy.*
Love does *not boast.*
Love is *not proud.*
Love is *not rude.*
Love is *not self-seeking.*
Love is *not easily angered.*
Love keeps *no record of wrongs.*
Love *delights in truth,* not in evil.
Love *always protects.*
Love *always trusts.*
Love *always hopes.*
Love always *perseveres.*
Love *never fails.*

2. Love One Another:

Circle the "one another" characteristic below you want to improve and make notes to the right about what you want to do to make that "one another" characteristic real in your life.

Encourage one another.
Build up one another.
Be kind to one another.
Live in harmony with one another.
Be devoted to one another.

Accept one another.
Serve one another.
Have concern for one another.
Carry each other's burdens.
Teach and admonish one another.

Pray for one another.
Don't judge one another.
Don't slander one another.
Don't provoke one another.

Speak truth to one another.
Be humble with one another.
Forgive one another.

3. Intentional Action – I intend to do the following:

____

____

____

Part II - Family

Chapter 4
Parenting Skills

"Parenting can be hard.
It's not particularly easy.
But it may be the most rewarding work
when it is done well."
Stephen H Berkey

INTRODUCTION

The basic fundamental responsibilities of a parent with regard to their children are to:

1. ***Explain*** the nature of life and the world.
2. ***Provide*** the necessities (food, shelter, clothes, etc.).
3. ***Protect*** from danger.
4. ***Instruct*** how to speak and communicate.
5. ***Supply*** knowledge and understanding.
6. ***Train*** how to use knowledge to make proper choices.
7. ***Teach*** right versus wrong (moral standards).
8. ***Discipline*** as necessary to reinforce all the above.

It is very easy for parents to focus on a child's success in school, in sports, and in extracurricular activities. Thus, it is not uncommon that parents forget the most important training—being a good person. Fighting the pervasive messages of instant gratification, consumerism, and selfishness in our society can be an extremely difficult challenge today.

If we want to raise good children, we must guide them in adopting habits and behaviors that promote positive character traits such as kindness, goodness, gratitude, and compassion. Being honest, living with integrity, and living a life based on truth must be the fundamental life principles taught by parents.

Raising a healthy and well-adjusted child is a challenging responsibility today. Most of us don't approach parenting with the same focus and intensity we use in our professional careers. We often act on our gut, personal logic, experience, or use the same parenting techniques as our parents. Unfortunately, this does not always produce the best results. Parents often use ineffective techniques and skills, simply because they don't know any better.

No matter your question, somebody has an answer. You can find good books on every parenting skill you want to know about. Therefore, as parents, you cannot claim there is no help being offered for the challenge of raising children.

Parenting styles

Training children to develop responsibility is one of the primary parenting goals. But poor parenting skills can often make that goal difficult. Poor parenting techniques can hinder a child from growing up knowing how to make good decisions.

There are many effective parenting styles. These styles can help ensure a parent maintains a good relationship with their children while teaching and training is occurring. The purpose is to produce the best behavior and good life habits. Although you may not be the perfect parent, strong parenting skills can prevent you from allowing your poor habits to control your parenting. Good parenting skills help you stay focused on your parenting. The parenting skills you use can bring out the best of both you and your child.

Does your child feel they are heard? Are you listening to their concerns? Do you spend enough time with your children, or too much time? Do they understand the purpose of the rules you establish? When you change your parenting approach or develop new techniques, does your child's behavior change?

"If you have never been hated by your child you have never been a parent."
Bette Davis

How to improve parenting skills

Even if you are a new parent and feel completely lost there are some simple techniques for developing and improving your parenting abilities.

First, **listen** to your kids. What are they complaining about? What gives them stress or anxiety? Make it a priority to talk with and listen to them daily. They are probably telling you something in all their complaining.

Second, **ask** them directly for input and feedback. What do they say they want? What do they say about your rules and boundaries? Do they have any valid points? Effective listening can help you determine how to do things differently and still achieve your objectives. They may have some good input, but remember you are the parent. If you get feedback from your kids, treat it seriously, so they know you care. But you make the decisions.

Third, your **body language** can easily be read by your children so don't send mixed signals. Your words should match your actions. Don't be hugging a child while you are punishing them. That can come afterward when the impact of the discipline has been absorbed or achieved.

Fourth, be sure that your instructions, rules, or **explanations are clear**. If your children don't understand, it will take much longer to change their behavior. Make sure your instructions are easy to follow. There is nothing more damaging than giving a child what they want after telling them no.

Fifth, **rules and boundaries** should be reasonable, age appropriate, and easy to obey. Don't make it complicated or the same for all children in the family. There is nothing more difficult to overcome than rules that are unreasonable or age inappropriate.

Sixth, don't be **hovering** over your children like a dark cloud waiting to correct some wrong behavior. Sometimes suffering the consequences can be a better teacher than your constant warnings.

Seventh, developing good parental skills and abilities takes **time and effort**. Seek advice from friends, parents, and books. There are many good books written about how to parent well. Your parents and other friends with older children have probably made all the mistakes you are facing. Don't hesitate to ask for advice.

Lastly, don't be afraid to **change** what you are doing. If some technique is not working, do something else. There is not one right way to be a good parent. Your children and their temperament will determine the appropriate type of parenting that may be necessary to successfully raise a particular child. It will also be necessary to change your approach as they grow and mature.

TWO KEY SKILLS

1. Communication

The best parents are frequently communicating with their children about all kinds of subjects. Communication should not be just about teaching and correcting. Parents should be talking with their child about everything. Ask them questions. Find out what they are wondering about.

Whenever a child presents you with questions, challenges, or school work, talk about it and what it means and why it is important. If they write, build, or draw something, talk about it. Complement them on what they have done and ask probing questions. You can praise them for their creativity but ask them why they did it, what they wanted to produce and whether or not they are satisfied?

Effective communication involves asking questions and conversing about subjects in order to not only help your children learn and understand new knowledge, but also to gain understanding about what they did, how they like it, and what they might change next time. It is important to help children understand their emotions and feelings about life as they relate to the projects they complete.

Talk to them about their likes and dislikes. Why do they enjoy doing certain things and not enjoy others? Keep your child engaged so that they can learn to communicate their feelings and thought processes. Make it easy for them to talk and ask questions.

Rules should be very specific in order to avoid confusion as well as frustration. If you want kids to go downstairs, don't ask them, "Who wants to go downstairs?" I used to get frustrated with my mom when she needed something at the grocery which was just a block away. She would ask me if I would like to go to the grocery. So after a while I said, "No, thank you." Don't be vague or ask questions when you should be giving instructions.

If your instructions, requests, or directions are not clear or are confusing, don't expect the kind of response you want. Yelling at children because they are confused or frustrated does not accomplish much.

"The trouble with learning to parent on the job is that your child is the teacher."
Robert Brault

2. Discipline

As a parent you're responsible for raising your kids and establishing the rules. How you deliver your instruction and practice your discipline will make a huge difference to your children. Do it with love and care, not with indifference. Avoid criticizing or fault-finding. Breaking down a child's confidence will almost always lead to resentment. Teach and encourage in the midst of correction. Make sure they know what you want and that you expect better next time.

One of the most important things children must learn is that everything they do or say has consequences (we discussed this in the Introduction). Consequences can be good or bad and the child needs to experience both. Do not overly protect your child from negative consequences. They must learn first-hand what happens when they make bad choices or fail at something. If Mom or Dad always protects them, saves them, or eliminates the possibility of negative consequences, the child may never learn that there are real consequences to their behavior.

Parents need to be aware of the nature of any offense and why it is occurring. Is the child trying to get your attention through their obnoxious behavior? Why is the behavior happening? Is it because the children are being kids or have they been ignored and need some attention?

Explain your rules and the reason for the discipline when it is imposed. Always carry out the consequences that you announced in advance. Never let children off the hook; otherwise they will continue to challenge you until you are forced to carry out some greater punishment. Make sure children understand why they are receiving punishment. Why do you want them to obey? They must clearly know why they are being disciplined.

Discipline your child consistently and with purpose. Parents who refuse to punish children for bad behavior or breaking rules are doing them no favors. In fact, lack of discipline can actually harm children. Your goal is not only to help your children learn self-control but for them to learn how to make the right choices.

Most children will test the rules and boundaries to make sure you are really serious. If the rules are appropriate, don't hold back on implementing your boundaries. Children need to understand your expectations. Immediate consequences for breaking rules will get attention and help establish that breaking rules can hurt. It is no different than choosing to walk across a busy street without looking. The consequences of getting hit by that car are far worse than a quick correction.

Be clear and concise

Don't give your child a long list rules to obey and expect them to conform. They cannot digest a long list of rules or requirements. Make your rules easy and simple to understand. Depending on their age and maturity they may need clarity and some practice before the desired behavior is established.

If your child goes into the back yard to play, make sure they understand the important boundaries for playing in the back yard. Every child is different but every child that goes out in the yard is going to get dirty, going to get a scratch, and going to try to leave the yard. Don't expect them to come back the way they went out.

Again, the rules and boundaries must be logical and meaningful. For example: no electronic devices until all school work is completed, no hitting, no name-calling, and no cursing. You will eventually have rules about bedtimes, curfews, type of clothing, riding with other teenage drivers, etc. Enforce boundaries when children are young so it won't come as a surprise when they're older.

Don't give your child any positive attention or reward for bad behavior. You will not get the behavior corrected until there are meaningful consequences. You can tell them afterward that you love them.

"Parents need to fill a child's bucket of self-esteem so high that the rest of the world can't poke enough holes to drain it dry."
Alvin Price

SKILLS YOU NEED FOR PARENTING

There are many skills that every parent might use at some time during their parenting. You could probably spend a lifetime reading books and blogs about parenting. There are also podcasts and webinars that can teach you anything you want to know. If you have the time, getting training can be very helpful, but it is time consuming and there is a lot of misinformation out there!

Depending on the training and the people doing it, it may be confusing. Every expert seems to have a different twist on the techniques for being a good parent. We are going to present the most important skills that you need to know about. Whether they are the best for you will depend on your personality and the temperament of your children.

Most of the following skills can be practiced by anyone. These are simple and easy to understand. You can integrate these techniques into your own parenting style.

1. Managing Children

Permissive parents can be overly lenient to their children's wants. They may give them nearly everything they ask for. This may result in the lack of consistent rules or boundaries. It may also produce family chaos and children who practically have more power than the parent. At the other end of the spectrum, authoritarian parents can be too strict and often very inflexible.

Being an involved parent does not mean doing everything for a child. You should never do their school work. You can give advice, but never do the work. If you do it, you have destroyed the learning dynamic. Prior to high school the primary focus should be on learning how to learn. Grades are not that important in these early growth years.

Independence and responsibility are desirable qualities that helicopter parenting can destroy. Instead of giving a child confidence, the helicopter parent overprotects the child and does not allow the child to see the real consequences of their behavior. Helicopter parenting prevents them learning on their own or understanding the implications of their poor decisions.

Parenting must also keep up with your child's development. The same techniques used at age 4 do not work at the age of 8. You should recognize the intelligence, curiosity, and temperament changes of your child. At some point your wonderful and beautiful child is going to get an attitude. Be ready for it! This too shall pass.

If a child doesn’t learn something quickly, it doesn't necessarily mean they are dumb or rebellious. They may just need more time. Be careful not to impose serious discipline on something that simply requires more time. Not every child learns certain skills at the same age or the same speed. Allow appropriate independence so that your child understands the impact of their words or actions.

Every parent has heard the famous words, “Trust me, pleeeese.” There will come a time when you need to let the child have their way even though you are pretty sure it will not end well. There is nothing wrong with this! Making mistakes is sometimes a very good learning experience. More is learned from mistakes than from success. If you make all the decisions, nothing is learned.

"Your children will become what you are; so be what you want them to be."
David Bly

2. Be a Role Model

You significantly influence how your children will act because they are watching you all the time. Model in word and deed how you would like your child to act. The younger they are the more they are learning. If you get frustrated and swear at your spouse, guess who is watching and learning from your behavior? You are constantly being observed by little brains that don't really understand adult behavior.

Therefore, model the behavior you wish to see in your kids: respect, humility, friendliness, honesty, kindness, goodness, etc. Don't expect your children to be unselfish if you act selfishly. If you do kind things for others, they will mimic your behavior. If you say "thank you" they will learn to do the same thing. If you swear at the driver in front of you, don't be surprised when they swear at you for doing something they don't like.

Children often begin copying a parent's behavior around the age of 3 (you can google it). If you allow your children to be exposed to negative behavior and bad habits, no matter the source, they will begin to exhibit that behavior. But don’t get to excited if you mess up once in a while. Everyone can do something they regret, just don't allow it to be a habit.

Being a good role model is not always as easy as it might sound. It can be easy to be pushed beyond your limit. Training children to control their limits is no different than trying to control our own. It can be difficult but it's important you are under control because they are watching you.

If you want your children to treat others with respect, you need to model that behavior for them. The most effective way to get children to speak and act respectful is to interact with others the way you want them to act. If you speak harshly or yell when you are not happy they will do the same.

3. Spend Time with Children

As children get older, have friends, and participate in school activities it is often hard for the family to be together for a family meal. You can wake up 10 to 20 minutes earlier in the morning and start the day together having breakfast. Make eating dinner together at night a priority even if it is difficult. At some ages eating together may be the only real time you have together.

Why is this important? Kids who aren't getting the attention they need or want often find ways to seek attention through their behavior. They know they will get some attention if they misbehave.

Some families create a "special night" each week to be together. You can let your kids decide how to spend the time. Make an effort to find ways to be together. Teenagers often seem to want less attention from their family. We are all very busy today with many kinds of activities and obligations. Parents do your best to be available when your kids want to be together.

Sometime the easiest time to get together is at school events where the child is present. Attending these activities with your kids communicates you care and allows you to relate to your child in their activities. You will also get exposed to the kids they tend to hang out with and be able to evaluate their choice of friends (a very valuable added bonus).

If you are a working parent it can be very difficult to participate in school activities. Don't feel guilty – that's life. In this case find other ways to be together: family nights, movie night, game night, etc. It is not always easy but it is critical that you make time for the important things in your life. Children grow up quickly and before you know it they are out of the house at college or married and living in another city.

You do not have to spend long and extended hours together. Sometimes an hour is more than enough if you are connecting with your kids, especially if it is on a regular basis. Make sure they feel loved and know you care. Here are some ideas how you might spend time together:

- Schedule weekly one-on-one time with each child.
- Play games that challenge their intellect.
- Tell them stories about family members.
- Encourage them to talk about their day.
- Take them along for errands or shopping.
- Participate with them in activities that are outside.
- Help them with school homework.
- Be present and celebrate birthdays and other successes in their life.

SUMMARY: Parenting is a big responsibility and you should plan and prepare for activities and learning experiences just as you would for a career. Children must learn what is safe and what can be dangerous. That can be as simple as how to choose good friends or be as complex as issues involving drugs or sexual activity. Your children will look to you first for guidance. Don't let them learn about life's dangers in back alleys. Be prepared to spend time teaching your children as well as having fun times in the activities you enjoy. Know what you want to accomplish and work hard at being a good parent while you are also loving, caring, and involved in their lives.

4. Rules

Not all rules, limits and boundaries are bad. Remember, you are the one with the knowledge and responsibility for training minds that are not fully developed. You are capable and able to make all the decisions they think they can make. You must teach them right and wrong, and explain the difference between what is good and why something is bad. You must prepare the child for the time when they must make their own decisions.

The rules and boundaries should be logical and reasonable. Rules enforced because "I said so," will not do much to help train a child. Rules are needed to teach good behavior and safety, not to give you time to rest.

As a parent you need to teach your child how to make good decisions and live with the idea they don't get everything they want. They must learn to live in community. Children with siblings find this much easier than children without brothers and sisters. An only child can sometimes find it overwhelming in kindergarten when they learn they are required to share!

Here are four guidelines for establishing good rules:

a. *Be consistent!* If you change the rules every week or only enforce them periodically, "Good luck!" Don't expect a child to obey rules that are not reasonable or enforced sometime.

b. *Be reasonable!* Don't make silly rules that are not logical and only for your benefit. Be wise on the use of rules and make them impact behavior, not create more tension because they are not understood or irrational.

c. *Explain your rules!* There can always be exceptions, but the child needs to understand the purpose and reason behind rules.

d. *Enforce behavior!* Don't expect anyone to follow rules that you do not enforce.

5. Love

You cannot spoil a child with affection. You can give them hugs and kisses without being concerned that you will spoil them. You can spoil them with unnecessary or extravagant gifts. You cannot buy love with things. A small child may be happy because you shower him with toys on every visit, but that charade will not produce love if it is not accompanied with true affection, caring, and love, which includes setting and enforcing rules.

The following acts will not spoil your child:

- time doing things together
- talking about important issues
- listening to their hopes, dreams, and problems
- celebrating their successes
- empathizing with their difficulties
- taking trips together

6. The Purpose is Good Behavior

Focus on the good behavior you desire, not on the punishment for the bad behavior. Focusing on punishment can sometimes lead to producing more bad behavior. Focus on what is desired and even consider appropriate rewards for success. You do not want your child to think they are inherently bad and there is no hope for them.

Recognize good behavior. Do not put all your emphasis on the bad behavior. You want your child to internalize the idea that they are appreciated and that the required good behavior is desired for their growth and maturity.

7. No Yelling

Yelling at kids is not the best way to communicate with them. Yelling is usually a knee-jerk reaction to your child's annoying behavior. Or, it may be necessary to send a warning! Yelling periodically to get attention is not necessarily bad, but if it is constant and overwhelming, it can encourage more poor behavior. Take time and walk away if necessary. You should not use yelling to make threats or accusations.

8. The Marriage is Paramount

Your marriage plays an important role in your relationship with your children. The less conflict in the marriage the easier it is to raise a normal or successful family. Solid marriages help produce well adapted children. This should not be surprising to anyone. If a child regularly witnesses fighting and bitterness in the marriage, that perspective will remain with the child forever. Good marriages generally produce good children.

9. Problems and Challenges

Successful people and marriages are not overcome by challenges. Although challenges can be difficult, do not shrink back from tough times. Real growth often occurs in the midst of challenges. Parents should influence their children's views about problems and challenges in a positive way. Challenges are a normal way of life and exist to be overcome.

10. Security and Safety

Children of all ages need to feel safe and secure in the family. Parents provide that security and safety in many ways beyond the safety of high walls and locked doors. "Safety" is also provided by:

- displaying affection
- saying words of affirmation and appreciation
- respecting their views and listening to them
- keeping your promises
- setting and keeping consistent boundaries
- reminding your child you love them, even when they fail at something
- encouraging participation, not necessarily winning

11. Manage Your Stress

Your stress can have an impact on your family and particularly your children. Children may not know what to call it but they know something is not right. You and I know that it is stress. If you are constantly stressed out or anxious, you will need to make a real effort to manage the challenges in your life that are causing that stress. Try to eliminate or reduce the things that create anxiety in your life. If conflict is the cause of stress, deal with it so that it is not a continuing factor negatively impacting the rest of your family.

Don't make minor situations that will go away into major issues (making mountains our of mole hills). Parents are not perfect. You have certain strengths and weaknesses that will not go away. Recognize who you are and play to your strengths.

Don't impose unreasonable timeframes on yourself or on your children. Don't try to do everything at once. Focusing on your needs does not make you selfish or a bad person. Care about your own well-being.

12. Talking and Listening

There is certainly a time for "lecturing" a child about their poor behavior and what and how they need to behave, but don't overdo it! Once a behavior event is over, that "lecture" should not be repeated every time you talk.

Some parents wonder why their children never talk to them. If your general response is to lecture your children about every topic they want to talk about, you can expect your conversations to dwindle to nothing. If you want to teach something, use the technique of asking questions. Ask why they think that way. Ask what they would do. Ask "why" questions. Don't tell them everything, rather help them come to the conclusion you want.

Children need to understand your values and beliefs. Why do you want them to act a certain way? Parents who reason with their kids allow them to gain understanding and gain wisdom in an atmosphere in which no one is being judged. You can even talk about potential solutions. Don't forget you are the parent. Children who participate in discussions about decisions are usually motivated to carry them out, unless they are using the discussion to stall off punishment.

If you don't listen actively to what children are saying you will likely miss some important clues as to what they are thinking. Have real "adult-type" conversations with them. What is on their mind and what are they worried about? If you ignore their desire to talk at a young age don't expect them to come to you as teenagers or young adults when they will really need your advice.

13. Praise and Reward

Encouraging words and rewards can be amazing motivators. Praise can often focus a child on their activities. Treats can be useful but should not be over used. The purpose is the right behavior, not the reward. Rewards can motivate them to achieve desirable behavior.

Rewards should not always be defined in advance. Occasionally surprise your child with a treat or give them a gift for good behavior. Special ice cream treats always worked well in motivating me! Kids love encouragement and thrive on parents' approval, so use it to your advantage. A reward also shows the child you care and appreciate their behavior. Celebrate achievements!

14. Flexibility

As your child grows and changes, you will need to change your parenting style and strategies. It is a sure thing that what worked with a younger child or another child will not work with the current one.

You must continue to hold to your core values regardless of outside influences. This may open up opportunities to talk about what is important in gaining maturity and why your core values differ from those of others. Take every opportunity to talk about core values and their importance in your family. The first core value you should teach your child is truthfulness. Honesty and integrity must be primary core values.

There will always come a time to expose the child to new challenges, activities, or responsibilities. Sometimes this is greatly desired by the child, but it can also be scary if the child is moving to an area outside their comfort zone. Don't push a child or be overly aggressive with new things; let them develop naturally.[23]

"There is no such thing as a perfect parent. So just be a real one."

Sue Atkins

SKILLS TO TEACH CHILDREN

Before we begin discussing specific skills, a word about feelings and emotions is necessary.

Emotional understanding, compassion, or the ability to put oneself in someone else's place is another one of the foundational aspects and character traits for being a good person. Being able to understand one's own feelings and recognizing the feelings and emotions of others is often important to unconditional love and forgiveness.

Encourage good personal character! Talk about feelings and emotions. If a conflict occurs with your child or if they have conflicts with their friends, make sure you talk about the feelings surrounding these conflicts. Help your child understand how they or others might be feeling. Talk about ways to show and handle emotions and feelings.

Remember, feelings and emotions are real. A child can have all kinds of fears or be fearless in situations where the reality is just the opposite. For example, they may not be scared of heights when they should be much more cautious than their feelings are telling them. On the other hand they may be truly scared of harmless spiders or bugs.

1. Empathy

Whether your children help the elderly neighbor next door care for their lawn, shovel a snowy sidewalk, or help you pack canned goods for a donation to the food bank, the act of volunteering or donating time helps shape your child's character. When children help others, they learn to think about the needs of the less fortunate. Unless they have real exposure to the disadvantaged it will be difficult for them to understand the life of the needy.

Children will often feel good about themselves when they help others. They even will give sacrificially because they do not assign the same value to money as most adults. Children can be very selfless, particularly if encouraged by parents or grandparents. If you want your child to feel like they have made a difference in the world, introduce them to the power of giving and sacrificing for others. Help them develop an interest in volunteering at a young age. Take them to the local food bank. Many children learn do good deeds for others in the normal course of their life.

2. Work Ethic: Chores and Responsibilities

Put your kids to work around the house. Children need to share in the responsibilities in the household. Chores teach diligence and resilience. These are valuable character traits to develop when young. Many important lessons are learned through chores. Kids learn to take responsibility and they can develop a strong work ethic. Understanding the meaning of "duty" and learning how to cooperate are also valuable skills that develop as the result of doing chores. Large families survive because the children share extensively in the chores.

Age appropriate chores such as helping set the table, sweeping the floor, mowing the grass, shoveling snow, or cleaning a room helps a child gain a sense of responsibility and accomplishment. Doing a good job and feeling they are contributing to the welfare of the household can significantly increase feelings of self-worth and being part of a family. Research has consistently indicated that kids who perform chores in childhood tend to become more successful as adults because they learn diligence and the value of work.

3. Social Skills

The earlier your child develops social skills, the better. Do not keep your child sheltered from other children or adults. It is important that they learn:

- truth telling
- conflict resolution
- cooperation
- politeness and kindness
- effective listening
- emotional control
- respect for others
- how and when to ask for help
- how to give effective feedback
- how to give compliments
- how to accept compliments
- gratitude sharing[4]

Parents should be on the lookout for times and situations when these skills can be taught. The age and maturity of the child should determine the timing.

4. Perseverance

Some believe grit and perseverance are more accurate measures of success than IQ tests. There are some very specific ways you can help a child develop perseverance and resilience:

- let them make mistakes
- model resilience for them
- focus on participation and learning rather than achievement
- teach the personal desire to overcome challenges and difficulties through hard work
- encourage them to accept reasonable risks
- mistakes and failures are not life-changing events, but giving up is not an attractive attribute[5]

5. Boost Your Child's Self-Esteem

A child gets their first clue about themselves from the words of their parents. Make sure that your words, actions, and body language send the right messages to little minds. They don't know you don't really mean the negative things you may say. They don't know you have other frustrations and the message they're receiving isn't actually about them!

Allowing children to make certain decisions can give them feelings of self-worth. However, if children are put down, belittled, or shunned, very serious damage can develop. Comparing a child unfavorably with a sibling or neighbor can also create feelings of worthlessness. Don’t say things like, "Well that was stupid!" Use mistakes or improper behavior as teaching moments.

Choose words carefully and show compassion. Mistakes are normally not earth-shaking and certainly should not send a message about the worth or value of a child. Disapproving their behavior should not send the message you don't love them.

Love and family light up the darkness.

Show children the love of family.
Love them as you want them to love you.
Be quick to forgive, don't hold grudges,
and seek reconciliation.
Speak kindness into the lives of your children.

CONCLUSION

As parents we cannot fall into the trap of indifference. We must love children and raise them up to be mothers, fathers, leaders, and statesmen. Parents are responsible for preparing the next generation.

Parenting may be one of the hardest but yet most rewarding jobs on the planet. We may question if we're doing it right or if it will make a difference. The secret is to persevere and do your best. We may not always be perfect but we can always give it our best.

We have a responsibility as parents. The important responsibility is to get children on the right path and it should not be taken lightly. We are responsible for training, coaching, instruction, correction, and discipline.

Discipline is an extremely important part of raising a child. It is not our intent to tell you what type of discipline should be used. It can be physical or not. The method is not the issue. The issue is effective discipline that produces the desired result. Discipline cannot be ignored because it is distasteful to you. Discipline will necessarily look different for every child.

We must be role models for our children. Everything we do or say will be seen and ultimately copied. They are observing everything we do and what appeals to them will soon appear in their behavior. They will try to copy the way we solve problems. They may even mimic the way we walk and talk. Whether we intend to set an example for children or not, they will be watching and doing exactly as we do. Thus, they will adopt our core values.

Setting a good example should be a priority. If you want to confuse your children, set up strict rules of performance and then don't conform to the same standards yourself. Saying one thing and acting another (hypocrisy) can do great damage to any form of child training and discipline.

Lastly, we as parents must supply what they need. They may not understand they need it and they might not want it, but parents have a responsibility beyond the desires or demands of the child. It's not making sure they have all the things you didn't get as a child. It is providing what is needed and necessary for their growth and maturity.

Raise your children to do the right thing, even when no one is watching!

Wisdom to Action Challenge

Evaluate your current parenting style. Are you prioritizing empathy, active listening, and unconditional support? Identify one area where you can enhance your positive parenting skills this week, and commit to consistent action in that area to strengthen your emotional bonds with your children.

Chapter 5
Disciplining Children

"Right discipline consists, not in external compulsion, but in the habits of mind which lead spontaneously to desirable rather than undesirable activities."
Bertrand Russell

To discipline a child means to train or teach them rules, boundaries, or morals to live by. This can be a very trying and stressful time for a parent. When you are just trying to keep a toddler alive and safe, the future value of what you teach them daily is often hard to keep in mind.

One of the frequent mistakes made by parents is thinking that your child will come to hate you for making them obey the rules. That is simply not true! Sadly many children ultimately resent their parents because they were not loved enough to be corrected and disciplined. Much of the depression and bad behavior of youth today could have been prevented if parents had loved their children enough to discipline them. Discipline is a matter of love!

PARENTAL RESPONSIBILITY

The parent's goal in raising children is to teach them that they can live independently when they leave home. The goal is that they are able to relate well with others, have a strong moral code and good core values, and have the strength to say no to peer pressure and other negative influences. Parents must teach their children that it is better to do what is right, even when there are overwhelming forces trying to convince them otherwise.

Teaching and training that is implemented with discipline starts when they are little toddlers. It begins with teaching obedience. And it never ends! Well, it does end in some ways but the feeling of love and responsibility never ends.

Obedience is the most crucial behavioral trait for the child's early life. The training in doing what is right begins as soon as the little minds of toddlers can comprehend and understand words and directions. The intent is to encourage obedience and the ultimate hope is that the child learns right from wrong and can make independent choices based on the core values you teach them.

If you have a strong-willed toddler you are undoubtedly going to have some long and frustrating days. The disciplining tips in this chapter will help you teach and train children whether they are compliant or strong-willed. You only have to persevere. Remember, your goal is to teach them right from wrong, good from bad, what constitutes dangerous behavior, and the guidelines the child needs to make good decisions. The ultimate objective is that they are a respected member of society.

There are several important principles to remember:

- Discipline does not necessarily mean punishment.
- You are the parent and the one responsible and in charge. You are not a best friend or pal.
- Instruction, correction, and discipline are not changed or modified because you love them.
- Punishment or correction should be administered by an adult family member, not a babysitter, friend, coach, teacher, etc.

If you do not handle a situation well the first time, don't hesitate to get advice and be willing to re-do or undo a situation that needs fixing. Correct your mistakes; don't let them continue simply because you are embarrassed to change your mind or change your methods.

If something should be done differently, do it now, don't wait for the next time. Maybe all you need to do is explain how the situation will be handled in the future. This not only fixes the mistake but tells your child you are reasonable and fair.

If someone tries to convince you that discipline is not necessary and the child will eventually figure it out, ignore that advice and be suspicious of the person's opinion about raising children. Good behavior does not just "happen." The purpose of discipline is to raise kind, good, respectful, and productive little people who will have upstanding qualities when they become adults.

It's normal to struggle and have many questions about the right kind of parenting and form of discipline you should implement. Ask for help. Do some reading and research. There are many sources of information on this subject. It is not surprising that large families seem to have an easier time raising children. That's because it takes a village and a large family is its own village. Take advantage of your extended family, your friends, your church, your community, etc.

As parents we may be anxious or stressed out about our children not liking us or being angry with us if we discipline or punish them. This can be heart-rending, particularly for some mothers with soft hearts and gentle spirits. You cannot let tender hearts determine your parenting style. Your objective is to raise a well-behaved child, not a life-long friend. Your child may not like your rules or discipline, but that is not the issue or the objective.

Should you physically discipline children?

It is not the purpose of this book to suggest what form of discipline you should exercise in your parenting. There are studies that suggest that spanking can have negative effects on children. Personally I see nothing wrong with limited and thoughtful corporal punishment.

Children are different and should be parented differently. You must decide what works best for you and your child. Our suggestion is that you refrain from automatically using the parenting style of your parents and educate yourself on the benefits of different parenting styles. But understand that angry responses and any form of abuse, physical or otherwise, are never appropriate.

Many people often want to know what the Bible says about physical punishment. Therefore, we have included information on that subject in Appendix B.

"Children must be taught
how to think,
not what to think."
Margaret Mead

DISCIPLINE STRATEGIES/TECHNIQUES

Following are a number of techniques you can choose to adopt as your parenting style. Explain to the child with calm clear words and actions what you are doing and why. Where possible, model behavior you want mimicked.

Always be clear about the behavior you want stopped. There should be no confusion or misunderstanding about what behavior is acceptable. Be flexible if appropriate, but don't allow any negotiation about the basics. Long debates, discussions, or arguments about discipline should not be allowed. Explain it, clarify it if needed, and end the discussion.

1. Specify clear limits

Have clear and consistent rules your children can follow. Be sure to explain these rules in age-appropriate terms they can understand. Make sure the rules are specific and cannot be misunderstood. If necessary give examples of what is acceptable and unacceptable behavior. Always explain why the rule exists.

The consequences should never be a mystery. Children need to know the consequences and parents must follow through with what has been established. If possible the consequences should be administered immediately. If you need to change the specified discipline, that change should take place the next time the rules are broken. Do not give second chances! There are no do-overs in parental consequences if you have set the rules and established them clearly in advance.

There are two important issues that you should follow:

> *a.* *Do not punish for something the child does not know is wrong.* If you make up the rules and consequences as you go along you will be viewed as unfair and unjust. You can even lose respect when you fail to carry out the specified consequence. There should be no, "Wait until your Dad gets home."
>
> *b.* *Be clear and consistent.* Consistency is often the secret to effective discipline. If you do not follow your own rules you set up, how can the child know that you are serious? If the "infraction" is not

exactly direct disobedience, don't be rigid unless the behavior is dangerous. If the child does something wrong and your rules are not clear or don't cover the actual behavior, don't automatically impose punishment. Always be consistent in administering the rules. Don't change the rules based on circumstances or because you are in public.

According to *PsychCentral*, parents may want to consider using their five C's, when establishing rules:

- **Clarity:** Ensure kids know the rules and there is no ambiguity.
- **Consistency:** Rules must always be enforced.
- **Communication:** Talk about the reasons for the rules and boundaries.
- **Caring:** When administering punishment, parents should be supportive, loving, and firm.
- **Create:** Teach children what right "moral behavior" is and what is expected of them.[6]

2. Clear and understood consequences

Fully explain the consequences of disobedience. If you cannot explain the consequence clearly and if it is not logical, you need to choose a more appropriate consequence. Make sure the consequence is permanent and lasts for the entire time you have specified. If you take something away from the child for a day, don't give it back after several hours.

If you tell a child to stop some behavior, you must make them stop! They cannot be allowed to continue the undesirable behavior until you lose patience. If some behavior must be stopped there should be some simple and easily defined time period for correction: (a) you can count to four, (b) you can specify that punishment will be administered if it occurs again, or (c) you can give them a two-minute timeout to calm down and get under control.

Obviously consequences should be real. Making a child stop and read a book they like is not very effective punishment. It should be something that they don't like, creates loss, or produces hurt. If you send them to the backyard to play on their toys, the punishment is not likely to be very helpful. If you use "time-outs" make sure the child is truly being punished. Some time-outs can give the child a time to rest and work up additional energy to continue to aggravate you more. Little is accomplished with timeouts that are not punitive.

Consequences should not only be clear, consistent and prompt, but it also cannot be too punitive or severe. Make sure the consequence fits the crime. The closer the consequences follow the misbehavior, the more likely they will be effective. Some children have a rather short memory and if the punishment occurs later, the chance it is very meaningful is highly unlikely.

If something is not allowed, it's not allowed. If you give in sometimes out of sheer exhaustion or because you weren't really committed to that rule, kids will pick up on that immediately. This means you need to choose and communicate your rules carefully.

According to *Evolve Treatment Centers*, when parents are clear about what the consequences are to kids, they have a better understanding of why rules are in place. Kids should recognize that it was their decision to break the rule and that they now face consequences. A child may not like the punishment but they should clearly understand the consequences are associated with their unacceptable behavior. The result will be better well-behaved children.[24]

FINAL CAUTION: Ignoring bad behavior (pretending you don't notice) means you are really encouraging it because there are no consequences.

3. Warnings

Don't be a parent who finally does something about your rules after 100 warnings. The child should know that they get one warning and no more. Never give more than one warning for anything. If you do it will delay the time it will take to teach the correct behavior. How often have you watched a parent repeatedly warn and threaten a child until they (the parent) finally reaches the breaking point and acts. It can be frustrating watching such a routine. You may feel like screaming at the parent, "Stop with the delaying routine and make him obey!"

When you want your child to do something, act as if you expect obedience. You can even give them some praise along with the commands. If the response is disobedience do the following – *every single time:*

- State the request clearly.
- If obedience does not occur, go to the child, and make eye contact, ask if the request was heard and understood.
- Repeat the command, and begin by saying, "Listen carefully to Mama/Daddy . . . "
- If the child refuses to obey, the punishment should fit the crime and it should occur immediately!
- Repeat the request after the punishment.
- Repeat the process if the child refuses to obey.[25]

The key here is being consistent. Immediate discipline is critical. This means you may have to do it in a public place and as long as physical punishment is not utilized, you will only receive looks of support. If your child tests you because they know you are in a public place don't panic or become frustrated. The child is hoping you cave. Once it is obvious you are serious, the testing will normally stop. That is likely only going to happen once or twice.

Another alternative for public displays of defiance is to take the child elsewhere or to the car. They lose the privilege of participating in the activity. This can be particularly effective if the remaining members of the family stay and participate in the activity.

4. Listen to complaints

Listen to your child's side of the story even if you know it's nonsense. They need to know that you are not unreasonable and there may be times when you missed something and grace is warranted. It may even be appropriate to respond to their side of the story, but this is not a negotiation or a debate. There should be no extended conversation and certainly no argument. The child may be trying to delay punishment or have your complete attention.

5. Give them attention

Some children can quickly discern that your time of giving training and discipline is a good time to spend time with you. Bad behavior should not be the catalyst for that attention. You may need to set up some special times during the day or week when they have your full attention without bad behavior! If your child appears to be acting up because they want your attention, that should be a clue that they need some of your time.

6. Compliment them

Children need to be told they did well. They want to hear that you are proud of them or that they did their best.

Reward them but don't accompany praise with additional instruction. That should occur at a later time. Just as you correct bad behavior you should encourage and reinforce good behavior. You can even be overly dramatic, particularly with younger children. Kids of all ages like praise and hugs (even though boys may pull away).

Do not encourage habits that give attention only to bad behavior. Give them attention when their behavior is normal. It may be necessary to wrap your arms around a child that is on the verge of losing their self-control. Tickle them or get them laughing in order to avert their attention from getting too excited or too focused on the wrong things. But do not ignore poor behavior for very long, it will simply encourage the child to continue such behavior.

7. Choose the best time to respond

Ignoring bad behavior can sometimes work but it usually is not effective in stopping behavior intended to get your attention. Obviously you cannot allow dangerous activities or sessions of poor behavior to occur. Choosing the right time to respond is often the key to effective discipline.

If they are doing something that destroys a toy, they will soon be without that toy. If they are throwing food they will soon be without food. If they refuse to wear their gloves, their hands are going to be cold. When children learn that behavior produces hurt, such behavior will normally stop. Suffering the natural consequences of a behavior is an effective teaching tool.

8. Are they just bored?

Sometimes children misbehave because they are bored and can't find something better to do. There is a very easy solution – find something for them to do! Yes, there are times you are their social coordinator and you need to point them to the obvious alternatives surrounding them.

It may be easier to redirect activity to other alternatives than to take a stand and declare your authority as the parent. But sometimes it is necessary! If you are saying no frequently, point them toward other activities. Humor and laughter are great alternatives for distraction. Direct them toward something fun. You might suggest going outside if a change of scenery is needed.

9. A time-out

Time-outs can be used for many purposes, including causing the current activity to stop. It may be time for a rest. It may be time for a snack. It may be time to practice the piano. You may want some job around the house completed. It may be a time for discussion and conversation about some activity or words that have been said. It may be a time of quiet or isolation. It may be standing in corner for 1-3 minutes. It can be anything that is effective in accomplishing the desired result: stopping the undesirable behavior. It should be short and age appropriate. This is not a time for argument or discussion.

10. Be realistic

Babies will cry, toddlers are going to investigate every place they can climb, young children will lie to avoid discipline, and teenagers will do almost anything that comes to mind. You cannot discipline a baby for crying because crying is a natural behavior. You cannot expect a toddler not to investigate their environment. And, you cannot expect a teenager to be perfect (or cooperative in some seasons of growth).

11. Model desired activities

If you want your child to read and enjoy the excitement of learning, you need to be seen reading books and talking about what you learned. If you want your children to have a quiet time, then they need to see you doing the same. You need to have priorities in your life that correspond to the habits you want to instill in your children. Otherwise, you will ultimately be viewed as a hypocrite and all the work and time you spent trying to instill what you say is desirable behavior will likely be lost.

12. Rewards

There is nothing wrong or improper with giving rewards for good behavior – just don't allow them to become bribes. The focus should never be on a prize and the reward should be secondary to teaching the correct behavior. Praise your children when you catch them being good and tell them, but don't sell and promote prizes for the right behavior.

13. Ineffective punishment

Remember the purpose of discipline is to teach children kindness, self-control, etc. It is not just to teach children to stop certain behavior. The purpose is to build a strong foundation for a loving and caring relationship, so the punishment utilized should not be overly harsh and should be appropriate for the nature of the offense. Ultimately the goal is for the child to discipline himself because he knows and understands that it is the <u>right</u> behavior.

If children stop certain behavior because they are afraid of you or because the punishment is particularly harsh, very little will be accomplished. Physical punishment can be helpful and useful, but punishment that is overly painful or humiliating can destroy self-esteem or create feelings of fear and hate. Choose carefully what punishment you select. Obviously the longer that physical punishment must be used the less likely it is being effective.

14. Discipline can be proactive

Proactive discipline means that you are is aware of the circumstances that might produce disobedience or poor behavior and you decide what you are going to do to maximize the teaching moment. This can be accomplished by planning activities where you have thought out ahead of time how the children should make good decisions. Thinking ahead can take more work, but it often will produce learned results more quickly.[7, 8]

CONCLUSION

There are five concepts that you should remember:

1. **Be Consistent**: Consistency is crucial in discipline. Children thrive when they know what to expect. Set clear rules and enforce them consistently. Avoid mixed messages or frequently changing the rules.

2. **Praise and Reward**: Focus on positive reinforcement rather than punishment. Reward good behavior. Celebrate small achievements and reinforce the desired actions.

3. **Be Age-appropriate**: Understand that children have limited impulse control and understanding of

consequences. Your expectations should match their age and development. Be realistic about what they can comprehend and manage.

4. Model the Behavior: Children learn by observing adults. Be a positive role model. Demonstrate respectful communication, empathy, and problem-solving skills. Show them how to handle emotions constructively.

5. Effective Communication: Use age-appropriate language to explain rules and consequences. Listen actively to their concerns and feelings. Encourage open dialogue and teach problem-solving techniques. Avoid yelling or harsh punishments.

Remember, discipline is about teaching and guiding, not just punishment. The objective is to help your child learn and grow.

"Self-discipline begins with the mastery of your thoughts. If you don't control what you think, you can't control what you do. Simply, self-discipline enables you to think first and act afterward."

Napoleon Hill

Wisdom to Action Challenge

Reflect on your current approach to discipline. Are you focusing on teaching rather than punishment? Identify one discipline technique you can implement this week that emphasizes guidance and positive reinforcement, and track the results of your consistent use of this method.

Chapter 6
Honor Your Family
(Parents – Siblings – Spouse)

***"Families are like branches on a tree.
We grow in different directions,
yet our roots remain as one."***
unknown

GENERAL

A couple had two little boys, ages 8 and 10, who were very mischievous. They were always getting into trouble, and their parents knew that if any mischief occurred in their neighborhood, their sons were probably involved. The boys' mother heard that a pastor in town had been successful in disciplining children, so she asked if he would speak with her boys. The pastor agreed, but asked to see them individually. So the mother sent her 8-year-old in to see him the following morning, intending to send the older boy in the afternoon.

The pastor was a large man with a booming voice. He sat the younger boy down and sternly asked, "Where is God?" The boy's mouth dropped open, but he made no response. The pastor repeated the question in an even sterner tone, "Where is God?" Again the boy made no attempt to answer. The pastor got to his feet. Shaking his finger in the boy's face, he bellowed, "WHERE IS GOD?"

The boy screamed and bolted from the room. He ran directly home and dove into his closet, slamming the door behind him. When his older brother found him a few minutes later, he asked, "What happened?" The younger brother, gasping for breath replied, "We're in big trouble! God is missing—and they think we did it!"[9]

This is a funny story, but what's the point in a book about love and family? If you are the parent what do you do next? What do you say to these boys that will be meaningful and teach them something? Did they get scared for a short time? Maybe! But if the older boy has any smarts, he knows God is not missing. But the story does have a point. Parents need to have a plan and know what they are doing when they train or discipline their children. The situation in this story probably did more harm in the long run and more than likely, it taught the boys nothing.

It's worthwhile to point out that a child with wisdom is more than just a smart kid. Wise people make good choices that produce good results. There is certainly the implication that wise children want to do what is right. In general, they should want to obey parents or caregivers. Foolish children, on the other hand, typically create difficulties for their parents and anyone acting as an overseer. Our goal as parents is to help develop understanding and wisdom in children.

Many proverbs and wise sayings speak directly about parents, children, and discipline. When we use the term discipline we do not necessarily mean punishment, but rather any act directed at helping a child gain control or knowledge through the use of instructions and rules that are to be obeyed. Discipline can also be described as the training that corrects, molds, or enforces obedience. There can be punishment and reward involved, but they are not the focus of the discipline; they are only tools.

Proverbial Wisdom

If we review the proverbs and wise sayings about family we could summarize their focus as follows:

- Parents discipline children because it is an act of love.
- Parents should diligently discipline children.
- Parents should not anger or abuse their children.
- Children have a duty to honor their parents.
- Children should learn from their parents' discipline.

Discipline is the responsibility of both parents and wisdom requires children to receive and respond appropriately to such instruction and correction. The purpose is that discipline produces knowledge and understanding. Failing to bring up children so that they know the difference between right and wrong can be a fatal mistake for both the parents as well as the children. The parent's responsibility might be summed up by the instruction: "Do not refuse to discipline a child – it may save their life!"

Wise sayings are very clear that children have the corresponding responsibility to honor their parents in receiving discipline. A foolish child avoids discipline and correction and does not learn from his mistakes. The goal of discipline is teaching and training in knowledge to gain understanding, which can lead to wisdom.

Young children are to honor their parents through their obedience and cooperation. How should adult children "honor" parents in ways that are fitting when they are no longer living at the home of their parents? We will discuss these questions and many more in the pages that follow.

HONOR YOUR PARENTS

How do we honor others? If you treat anything else (people, hobbies, work, etc.) better than you treat your family, you are not honoring them. Some people tend to treat their neighbors and friends better than their own family. They would do anything for a friend but neglect their family.

Honoring parents means that you treat them as well as anyone else, and even better, because they are parents. In reality you should treat your family better than others, and you should give more importance to the needs of your family as compared to others. If you do this, you are honoring and respecting their position as parents.

There is some thought that in order to honor your parents you must obey their wishes, and particularly those of the father. Does this mean you have to agree or do everything they want? No! But being obstinate and uncooperative is not a good alternative.

Honoring doesn't mean agreeing. It means respecting. If you are annoyed by your parents nagging you about something, make sure that it is not because you are failing to "honor" them. Generally, parents want to know that you care and will be there for them if they need your help.

"Family is not an important thing. It's everything."
Michael J. Fox

How does an adult child "honor" a parent?

The challenge to honor parents can be summarized by the following four concepts:

a. **Appreciation.** You honor parents when you appreciate what they have done for you. You show your appreciation by valuing or listening to their guidance and advice. It does not mean that you must act on their advice.

b. **Authority.** When you are young you honor your parents by recognizing their authority in your life. You should be obedient and cooperative. If you are newly married, parents should not try to control or manage the marriage. Married couples certainly benefit from the advice of parents but, a married couple may decide to set boundaries limiting the involvement of relatives in their marriage.

It is certainly not true that parents or in-laws have any authority in their children's marriage. All the authority rests with the married couple, but that does not mean that good sound advice should be ignored in a show of independence. Remember, parents probably made the mistakes you have made or are thinking of making.

c. **Respect.** This can often include both what you say and how you say it. Avoid disrespectful speech and actions. Speaking abusively to parents is not helpful or attractive.

d. **Provision.** When your parents get old, they may need practical support. You can honor them by trying your best to make sure that they have what they need. They may also require help physically as they age and cannot perform certain functions well, if at all.[10]

"The best way to honor your parents is by being the best version of yourself." Unknown

What honor doesn't mean

Honoring means giving respect, admiration, or just plain being nice. It's also important to recognize what honor does not mean. It is sometimes easy to hear something that's not being said. Let's be clear about what honoring does not mean.

Logical disagreement is not bad. It only means you have a different opinion. It says nothing about your character. Disagreement only becomes bad if you stubbornly refuse to listen to anyone else or refuse to evaluate their thoughts or ideas. Disagreement does not mean you disrespect the other party. It does not mean you are angry with someone. It certainly does not mean or imply rebellion of any kind.

Some people have the idea that to honor and respect parents, adult children must always do what the parents want. Taking the advice of parents should always be taken based on the quality of the advice. Who would you prefer to hear from when you have gotten off track, a loving family member or a business associate?

Honoring family doesn't mean we always support family decisions, but we have their back in all situations, because they are family. Our own family should be the priority in our lives. Our spouses are a priority. Our children are a priority. Our parents can be a priority. It is not complicated, although we can make it that way if we lose sight of respect and honor in family relationships.

Why honor and not love?

We should remember the cultural context of the times when this commandment was first given. Honoring one's parents was seen as a fundamental virtue and a key to maintaining social order. Life existed in the context of family. It was not only about affection but also about acknowledging the role of parents as authority figures and providers. It emphasized the importance of familial relationships while supporting ongoing societal stability.

The use of the word "honor" in this context carries a broader meaning than just love. While love would be an important aspect of the parent-child relationship, honoring one's parents involves showing them respect and obedience in a culture dominated by the family unit. Honoring implied recognizing the cultural value, authority, and control of parents and elders in the family hierarchy.

Summary

Parents often get a reputation they do not deserve. TV shows and movies, particularly sit-coms, make use of ugly family situations and dynamics. These often become accepted truths although they only occur in the minds of sit-com writers. Yes, there are dysfunctional families in the world, but they should not impact our relationship with our own family members. This does not mean that you live in denial of hurtful situations, but do not allow society to dictate how you treat your parents and family members.

"Honor your parents by listening to their stories, for they are the roots from which you grew."
Unknown

What about terrible parents?

Let's face it, not everyone has a good family or parents who deserve being loved. You may have been raised under terrible circumstances by stand-in or actual parents. When you hear the phrase "honor your parents," your stomach churns just thinking about paying tribute to someone who treated you badly. It may not be easy or even possible to honor someone who has hurt you so deeply. I am sorry for your circumstances, but I can tell you that to repay evil for evil, hold a grudge, or seek retribution will not serve you well. You are the one carrying the baggage. Put it down.

Caring for parents who never cared for you has nothing to do with helping them, but everything to do with helping yourself. For your own peace of mind, do it so that you never have to live with regret. Even if you don't care about the people who weren't there for you, when they're gone you may feel differently. By then, it'll be too late. It is never wrong to do the right thing. No one ever regrets taking the high road.

WHY HONOR PARENTS?

Our parents cared for us for the first 15 years of life and we are likely going to need to care for them in the last 15 years of their lives. It is the nature of life. It's family.

Our parents deserve the best we can do for them in this life. They generally made significant sacrifices for their family. Caring about themselves is often not on their priority list. Most parents desperately want their children to have a better life than they themselves experienced. This is a natural feeling of love for children because they want them to live their best life.

Yes, some people were terrible parents. In some cases children want nothing to do with parents who treated them badly or just didn't care. I think that is one of the reasons the commandment in the Bible is to honor and not to love. Children have an inherent and fundamental family obligation to parents, no matter how well or bad they were parented.

Parents have an inherent responsibility

In a broader context parents are given both authority and responsibility to raise children in such a way that they are honest and upright. Parents obviously have life experiences and knowledge they can transfer to children. That means children are to be taught right and wrong, and what is good and what is bad.

But whether parents manage their responsibilities as parents in a good, bad, godly, or ungodly manner, it doesn't change the responsibility of the children. Children are called to honor and respect parents based on their *position* as parents.

Our parent's responsibility is to teach us, protect us, and provide for us. When appropriate we must return the favor. If you do not think this is a general law of nature, look around at the situations you know about where children dishonored and disrespected their parents or family. How is life going for them?

Have you ever compared your parents to other parents? Maybe you've even verbalized that thought. You may even think God or fate made a mistake when your parents arrived on the scene! But we probably need our parents more than we think. Have you ever seen a newborn? How about a puppy? Babies can't eat, drink, walk, or talk. They can't even hold up their heads. All they can do is cry, laugh, smile, and sleep. Puppies can't see or hear when they are born. In both cases, these newborns need help, training, and discipline to mature physically and mentally.

WAYS TO HONOR PARENTS

When we enter this world we are helpless, in fact, initially we are so helpless we would die without parents. We can't feed ourselves, communicate, or do anything for ourselves. We sleep, eat, and get rid of what we eat, that's about it. Our parents spend the first five years trying to make sure we survive. Then for the next 5-15 years we drive them crazy with our antics, rebellion, and demands.

To honor your parents begins by being thankful for them. In looking back over those early years you can almost feel sorry for them. You have to wonder if they ever imagined the trouble we were capable of creating. Luckily not all children are terrors and there exists within most parents and inherent love for a child that nothing can destroy.

It doesn't take a lot of energy to come up with everything your parents might have done better. Parents are never perfect but most did the best they could do. Everyone has redeeming qualities. If you think your childhood was not the best, then try to think of or remember the good moments during your childhood. What positive qualities or attributes did your parents give you? Did they positively shape your personality? Consider how your parents provided for you and trained you to survive on your own.

Honor implies giving something of value. The value of our parents is incalculable in many ways. We were created to have relationships with others and your parents are the first deep relationship that occurs in your life. If your childhood was bumpy, remember your parents did not choose your personality and temperament. Likewise, you did not choose your parents. It was simply a matter of the miraculous birth process.

Communication

Honoring parents requires that you communicate with them, even if it is only to ask how they are doing and what is going on in their lives. Show interest in their lives and they are likely to do the same with you. Ask questions about what is challenging for them in their current circumstances. How could you help them? Family has the responsibility to care for and watch out for each other whether it is siblings or parents. In order to do this there must be open lines of communication. You need to talk to family more than once a month! A visit is even better.

Whether you want to recognize it or not parents have a great deal of knowledge and experience that can be beneficial in your life. There's a great deal we can learn from past generations. They can help us avoid pitfalls and mistakes that they experienced. It is very easy to make the same mistakes when we do not have the advice of parents that had the same questions or challenges when they were young. Elders can often provide great insight, but you have to talk to them to hear the advice.

As parents age it is often wise to talk with them on a regular basis. This can be a minor inconvenience for you but it may be the highlight of their week. Unfortunately, sometimes it may be the only conversation they have from week to week.

Do not underestimate the value of talking, sending letters, or even texting. Communication is the foundation of a relationship. If you do not communicate, you cannot connect. We are not honoring parents when we ignore them or cut them off with unkind words. Remember, how we communicate to family is an indication of how we really feel about them. Our words must honor them as well as our actions and body language.

When I remember some of the things that I said and did when I was a teenager (and became all-knowing), I wonder how I survived! I was too young and immature to understand what I was doing and saying. Did you ever have times like that? I always remember the story about the twenty-something that wakes up one day and wonders how their parents became so smart all of a sudden. Duh! I have heard it said that teenage girls can be particularly wretched to their mothers. When that begins to happen it is time for Dad to step in and explain the facts of life to the child. You can talk to them and they can understand!

Remember, parents and children probably know each other better than anyone else. You may have lived together for twenty years and experienced every sort of problem and challenge during those years. You know each other in ways nobody else could possibly understand.

Truth

One of the most important rules of any family relationship is truth and integrity. Lying to parents has been going on since time began. You might be totally surprised by how many children lie to their parents. Why? Normally such behavior is because children fear the consequences of their behavior. Some probably don't want to disappoint their parents. The lack of truth and honesty can be a serious hurdle in maintaining good family relationships.

Relationships cannot survive if they are built on lies, deceit, or cheating. I should stop at this point and state bluntly that if your relationship with a parent or child is built on lies, confess the truth to them and ask them to forgive you. You honor your parents or child by speaking the truth. Live your life based on honesty, integrity, and the truth. Anything else will haunt you as long as untruth is the basis of a relationship.

Respectfully disagree, if necessary. There may be times when you totally disagree with your parents or children. They might be completely wrong about something. You honor them by being true to your core values. That does not mean that you are disrespectful or abusive. Both parents and children must be allowed to make mistakes. But you do not have to condone or agree with their choices. You must continue to treat them as loved members of the family while being honest.

Obviously parents have lived longer lives and experienced much more than children or young adults. Parents likely experienced much of what their children will face in their early years. Let's face it, young people can be foolish. Unfortunately that foolishness can be dressed in the clothes of excitement, opportunity, or the promise of easy riches. Asking parents or elders for advice varies greatly in some cultures. It might be expected or it might happen only at the request of the child. Regardless, the one asking for advice honors the one asked.

Mothers

Don't exclude your mother from your life. Don't exclude your father either. Remember, relationships are not the same for men and women. Adult children can often talk with fathers monthly or yearly and everyone is satisfied. That is not true for mothers. Women are inherently more relational and need or want more communication.

Let's be real: mothers generally took care of the children and often provided a different degree of guidance, protection and warmth. Thus, as children grow up and begin to leave the nest, the feelings can be intense. Suddenly the relationship is no longer needed or desired. The relationship is no longer what it used to be and when marriage occurs, the entire relationship changes again.

"The heart of a mother is a deep abyss at the bottom of which you will always find forgiveness."
Honoré de Balzac

Encouragement

Encouraging your parents, particularly in their later years, is a wonderful way to honor parents. Obviously, their age, health, careers, education, and interests, all play an important role in what would be appropriate encouragement. If your parents are educated, skilled in communication, or very outgoing, you could encourage them to share their wisdom or skills with younger men or women. They might participate in Big Brother/Big Sisters or be mentors to younger adults in need of guidance.

If because of life circumstances your parents must depend on you more than normal, do all you can to ensure they don't feel they are a burden. Your unconditional love can help them avoid depression or despair. The cycle of life that provides for parents to care for helpless children can come full circle when the children are caring for parents who need help. Choose to focus on the good things in life and be a source of light, not darkness.

Forgiveness

It is often necessary to honor parents through forgiveness. Forgive them for anything they did that pushes your buttons. All parents make mistakes? There are no perfect parents, but some are better than others. All have made choices they probably wish they could make over.

Being mired in anger, bitterness, and resentment is not a good place to be and will not fix a situation that can probably be resolved with the words, "I'm sorry."

Extending grace is far more helpful than hoping the problem will go away. Time does heal many wounds, but don't spend time being anxious or upset when something can be resolved with a few kind or forgiving words.

Forgiveness might be the most important act we perform in an ongoing relationship with parents and family. We all fall short of being the perfect parents or children and we often wish we had done better. Everyone makes unwise choices and we can think that parents should always make the right decision or give the best advice, but that is not realistic. Poorly chosen words or reactions made in the heat of any discussion can be devastating and cause serious problems. If deep wounds occur in the early years of childhood and particularly during the teenage years, it may be extremely difficult to get over the hurt.

Caring for parents

Taking care of your parents can be as simple as driving or accompanying them to the grocery store and helping them shop. But it can also mean you have to help and advise them about questions of health or financial security. Ultimately it may mean that children must be prepared to do things for their parents that they can no longer do for themselves. That can involve their physical, mental, and even their emotional and mental stability. That may sound a bit scary, but it is not any different from what they did for you as a child when you were not old enough or mature enough to do it for yourself.

Model the loving and honoring behavior to your parents that you would wish to receive from your children. Here are two areas where special concern may be necessary:

Supporting their needs

As parents age they typically become more feeble. They may lose the ability to live independently. We honor them by giving them the assurance that we will not forsake or abandon them. Just as they cared for us, we will care for them. It is not only a family responsibility but it should be a source of joy to serve the needs of parents. Living alone in a nursing facility and being cared for by strangers is not a particularly attractive outlook, although sometimes it is unavoidable.

Being helpful and compassionate

Has anyone ever extended you mercy or compassion? Have you ever received something you did not deserve? Did you appreciate that compassion? The next time you are hurt by a parent, extend mercy and forgiveness. Be compassionate! Take the high road. Put aside any bitterness and intentionally extend grace.

Honor, love, and grace can tear down mountains. Remember, as people age their capabilities and social interactions may suffer. Losing the ability to think correctly, communicate effectively, and take care of oneself is frustrating for a parent.

Public and private support

You can honor your parents simply by the way you speak of them, both publically and privately. Praise them whenever the opportunity arises.

The internet and social media make it easy to say things digitally that we would never say face-to-face. Some people seem to live to air their grievances or hate on social media platforms. But that does not honor anybody! Our words have the power to extend both honor and dishonor. To curse or belittle someone is not honoring.

Talk about problems and issues

If there are problems you may need a plan, particularly if your situation is very difficult or awkward. You may want to establish some ground rules. Sit down with your parents and ask them questions like:

- What is most important in our new relationship?
- How do you think we should handle areas of potential conflict?
- What is most important to you?
- What is not important to you?
- What family traditions, activities or events are really important to you? (Ask about holidays, vacations, birthdays, etc.)
- What kind of relationship do you want with your grandchildren? How often do you want to see them? Would you enjoy babysitting?

When you have these discussions you can find alternatives and possible solutions. But you may have to compromise.

There may be times when you must gently correct your parents, especially if their incorrect thinking could create serious problems. Such correction should be bathed in love, kindness, respect, and patience. Parents deserve the right to know the truth. They can then choose to heed or disregard it.

"There is no doubt that it is around the family and the home that all the greatest virtues of human society are created, strengthened and maintained."
Winston Churchill

WAYS TO SHOW LOVE TO FAMILY

How do you show love to your parents? Obviously the answer to this question will vary significantly depending on your age and maturity. Let's assume that you are not a parent yourself. This means you may have some trouble understanding the love, worries, stress, expectations, and longings that a parent might feel.

What might be important to the parent can often have little interest to the child. Remember, the entire perspective of the parent and child is totally different during the formative dependent years. It is not easy for either a parent or a child when the relationship begins to change. Some parents may have sacrificed a great deal while others not so much. Relating to each other as adults after twenty years of an adult/child relationship is sometimes a tough change for both the child and parent.

Spend time

There is more desirable for a parent than a child who offers his time and presence. But that requires effort and the requirements for such a relationship change as the child matures and leaves the home. Parents often want to talk but they don't really need advice; they just want someone to listen to them. Can you be a good listener?

If distance permits, check in personally with parents periodically. It does not need to be a long visit. All you need to do is show up, show interest, and check on any special needs. If a visit isn't possible, a phone call will do. Today you can even chat by video and observe body language and subtle communication clues.

Communication between family members is the number one requirement for a healthy family atmosphere. Whatever you do to have fun, include them in those activities, as long as it is not overly strenuous or taxing. Watch a movie with them or discuss a book you have read with them. Take them shopping. Include them in your routine activities as appropriate.

Make them feel important in your life. Give them your full attention. Let them feel that you are eager to listen to them, no matter how busy you are. Ask for advice. Demonstrate that you value their opinion. If you have children already, your mom and dad would surely love to have their grandchildren around. Even let them spoil your kids on occasion.

Special occasions

On special occasions, such as, Mother's Day, Father's Day, and birthdays give them something that is thoughtful or useful. Make sure they are invited to Thanksgiving dinner and Christmas.

Positive attitude

Don't be rude or disrespectful. It will accomplish nothing and worsen your relationship. What you can expect to receive from disrespect is disrespect in return. Arguing or fighting about some issue is generally not going to resolve a disagreement. A calm discussion where both parties try to understand the concerns of the other is more likely to reach a compromise than yelling or mean words.

Parent's claiming they are the boss (even though that may be true) and children claiming they are being mistreated (and that may also be true) is usually not a place in which a reasonable resolution can be reached. The power dynamic between parents and children can be very challenging

If you disagree with a parent, demonstrate that you are interested in talking or listening to them. Avoid exhibiting signs of boredom or impatience (looking at the ceiling, checking your watch, or looking at your phone) while they are talking. If you are not going to pay attention to them, don't expect them to pay attention to you.

Some parents may want to try to take care of children even though the child is an adult. You may not even be living at home. Just know that they will always think of you as their child and want to help and protect you – that's what a parent does. They love you. Therefore, honor them in return.

"Our most basic instinct is not for survival but for family. Most of us would give our own life for the survival of a family member, yet we lead our daily life too often as if we take our family for granted."
Paul Pearsall

HONOR YOUR PARENTS WHILE YOU CAN

Let's be very real. You can lose your parents at any time. It is so sad to be estranged from family and after a death be grieved because you never made things right between you. Many regret for the rest of their life they never took the time to resolve relationships. That opportunity can be gone in an instant.

Many people end up regretting things left unsaid, time wasted, and forgiveness left ungiven. That is so sad since just a little bit of grace and love could have resolved the situation, or could resolve it now.

The real question is how you want to live your life now. You can refuse to ask for or grant forgiveness. You can hope they will begin treating you differently. You can hope for miracles! You cannot act as if the past never happened, but you don't have to live in a state of anxiety and stress about the future. Simply decide you are going to honor them in your life regardless of their attitude. Honor them the way you wish they'd cared for you. Do this for your own well-being, not for theirs.

Remember, being a good person is about how you treat them, not how you feel about them. You can honor them through simple acts of kindness and respect.

Love versus like

We are suggesting that your calling as a child is to honor parents, not necessarily to like them. What does that mean? If you honor parents you give them respect. You treat them with dignity, regardless of how they may have treated you or the state of your current relationship.

Some children today believe their parents owe them in some way. They believe that what the parent owns is theirs (children will inherit it in future anyway).

But there is a bigger truth in the wisdom of the proverbs and wise sayings. They teach that children should not disgrace or shame the family. The proverbs caution that foolish words and actions can destroy a family.

There is an African proverb that says, "The child who is not embraced by the village will burn it down to feel its warmth." Children need and want the warmth and guidance of the family to encourage and love them through both the good and bad times. That need can be so strong that it can produce foolish behavior in order to gain the attention of parents or other adults.[11]

"A parent's love is whole no matter how many times divided."

Robert Brault

CONCLUSION

We have a great deal to be thankful for when we consider the contribution of good parents in our lives. Parents help us grow physically, emotionally, and spiritually. Without them we wouldn't survive. We are literally dependent on our parents for our being, who we are, and likely who we will become. Consider the following:

1. Your parents loved and cared for you.
2. Your parents raised and provided for you.
3. Your parents trained and guided you.
4. Your parents encouraged you.
5. Your parents gave you hope.
6. Your parents were merciful to you.
7. Your parents blessed, protected, and sheltered you.
8. Your parents warned you of danger.
9. Your parents imparted understanding to you.
10. Your parents listened to you.
11. Your parents talked and read to you.
12. Your parents sacrificed for you.
13. Your parents enjoyed you.
14. Your parents forgave you.
15. Your parents challenged and tested you.
16. Your parents helped bear your burdens.

17. Your parents corrected and disciplined you.
18. Your parents were patient with you.
19. Your parents gave generously to you.
20. Your parents patched you up and comforted you.
21. Your parents influenced and inspired you.
22. Your parents prepared you for the real world.
23. Your parents confronted you.
24. Your parents praised you.
25. Your parents cried and rejoiced with you.
26. Your parents cherished you.
27. Your parents offered you advice.
28. Your parents held you accountable.
29. Your parents told you the truth.
30. Your parents invested in you.[12]

PERSONAL CHALLENGE: See if you can remember and note opposite each of the activities above a time and occurrence when your parents performed the act described.

"The greatest gift you can give your children is to believe in them."
Zig Ziglar

Wisdom to Action Challenge

Consider your relationship with your parents. Are you treating them with respect, appreciation, and provision? Identify one specific action you can take this week to honor your parents, regardless of their past actions, and reflect on how this act impacts your inner peace and relationships.

Chapter 7
Children, Listen to Your Parents!
(Obedience and Respect)

"Parents were the only ones obligated to love you; from the rest of the world you had to earn it."
Ann Brashares

INTRODUCTION

The big complaint about parents from teenagers is that parents do not understand them. Thus, the child's life becomes an uphill battle to achieve any sense of joy, satisfaction, or contentment. Most parents love their children and want the best for them, so the complaint does not hold much water as a general truth. Simply because parents have rules and want to teach children the correct or appropriate behavior is not a valid reason for claiming parents don't understand them. The truth is they probably understand them all too well because they were teenagers once themselves.

Sometimes the accusation is that parents do not respect their children. But respect is more about abilities and capabilities than an issue of love or relationship. It can be said that I respect a coworker, even though I do not agree with his ideas or beliefs. In fact I can respect him and think he is absolutely wrong. I can respect others, including my children, and not have any obligation to do something for them, agree with them, or give them anything. Respect is like a reputation: you earn it through your actions. The person wanting to be respected or honored needs to earn and deserve that type of recognition. It is not given simply because someone exists. Neither is it purchased or received because of some quid pro quo.

Obedience to parents is normal and expected. Obeying parents demonstrates you have been taught and trained in proper and expected behavior. Obedience will often gain children respect from other elders. Obedience to parents comes with many benefits to children from both family and other adults. It signals loyalty and a degree of wisdom to those watching. Adults outside the family are attracted to children who honor, obey, and respect their parents or other elders, particularly those in authority. It demonstrates a desired degree of maturity.

Other adults will usually help children when needed if they have been helpful, respectful, and kind. If you are an aggressive bore as a child, don't expect adults to come running to your aid. Calls for help might even be considered ploys to gain some advantage or freedom that is undeserved. Adults who observe respectful behavior can be called on to help mentor or train children in special skills. Adults are usually reluctant to teach skills to disrespectful children.

WHY DO CHILDREN DISOBEY?

Do you ever think about why a child disobeys? Why did you disobey your parents? Why do children take a position that seems to be clearly contrary to what would be right? Here are some of the common reasons children disobey:

Tension or stress: Children can suffer from stress just like adults. It can be produced by difficult situations in the home, extended family, school, church, neighborhood, or workplace.

Anger or revenge: Anger can result from rebellion against the authority of a family member or friend. It can result from anger directed against the family because of perceived or actual poor treatment.

Unknown reason: Children can disobey because of past situations that they witnessed, overheard, or experienced. Such incidents may be totally unknown to the parent. For example, the parent may not know about sexual abuse of the child or their sibling, trouble at school, or relational problems with the child's friends.

Willfulness: Children may disobey because they are stubborn, rebellious, or even vengeful. The child may choose a path of rebellion or to exercise their own strong will in spite of proper parental teaching and modeling.

Jealousness: Children may create or even desire chaos when they feel they have been treated unfairly, cheated, or are out of favor with the family. They may feel they have been punished unfairly and held accountable for something out of their control. If they are strongly admonished in public they can have feeling of shame and revenge.

There are a large number of wise sayings and proverbs that instruct children how to act. We have summarized and combined that wisdom into six important instructions to children:

1. Listen to your parent's instruction, teaching, correction, or rebuke.
2. Don't depart from or ignore wisdom taught by teachers and other leaders.
3. A wise child will bring honor to his parents.
4. A good child is prudent and diligent, not foolish.
5. Don't be lazy or apathetic.
6. A bad child causes grief and distress in the family.

Making the right decisions and learning good habits and behavior as a child will influence decisions when children are older. Children need to gain basic knowledge and understanding about right and wrong when they are young. Parents can be a source of wisdom based on their experience long after the child is on their own.

Much can be learned from correction and it is the wise child, not the rebellious one, who understands the value of instruction and even rebuke. The rebellious child is generally not genuine or sincere and will often criticize or belittle others who learn from their mistakes.

It is said that a discerning child will obey. To be a discerning child means that one is able to understand and accurately evaluate the situation. He understands the need for rules and chooses to obey them because it is to his ultimate benefit. For example, a discerning daughter would not get into a car alone with a group of boys. A discerning son would know not to get into a car with friends who have been drinking.

The bad behavior of children caused by the influence of poor companions or associates will humiliate or greatly disappoint parents.

"The object of teaching a child is to enable him to get along without his teacher."
Elbert Hubbard

CHILDREN CAN DISHONOR PARENTS

What could a child do that might dishonor their parents? The easy answer is anything that causes grief. Often it is simple disobedience. But it can also be actions that bring disgrace or shame to the family name. Here are a number of ways that children can dishonor parents. We think these are self-explanatory and do not need further discussion.

- Failure to obey parents.
- Being disrespectful and swearing at parents.
- Speaking evil of parents.
- Hitting parents.
- Being rude and talking back to parents.
- Stealing from parents.
- Lying to parents.
- Yelling at parents.
- Being rebellious toward parents.
- Posting insulting comments on social media.
- Sneaking friends in the house without permission.
- Continually complaining about parents.
- Rolling eyes at parents.
- Ignoring parents when they ask questions.
- Being arrogant or a know-it-all.
- Have arguments that cause hate and anger.

While children should obey their parents, parents should not provoke their children to anger. Children and parents all make mistakes. We all can fail in our roles in many ways. It behooves both children and parents to work together in harmony to produce a loving and supportive family atmosphere.[13]

"Children are like wet cement. Whatever falls on them makes an impression."

Dr. Haim Ginott

RESPECT YOUR PARENTS (and all elders)

The first question a child might ask in response to this heading is why? There are a number of very logical reasons why respect is appropriate.

Parents are older and wiser. It's not really about age, but older people have lived life and gained understanding and wisdom from the challenges they have experienced. Children can gain much if they have parents who will share their experiences, both good and bad. These experiences help guide children in making good decisions. Be sure to ask parents how and why they did what they did. What would they now do differently, and what would they specifically do in your case?

They have sacrificed for their children. While you were a baby and a toddler they spent most of their total life providing for your needs. As you became older they provided for your future and well-being. It is really overwhelming to think how much time and effort parents invest in their children. Now it is time to begin returning the unconditional love you received.

They know everything about their children. Who else could possibly know you any better than a parent? Of course they know you better than anyone else! They were there during all the challenges, successes, and failures. There is no one who has the insight to advise and help you more than your parents.

Life is sweet when parents are honored by their children. Remember, honor and respect are earned. They cannot be given as a gift or unwillingly. Respect is given because someone treats another well, helps or cares for another, or does something for another. It is not always because great things or results were accomplished. It can be the simple result of love. Respecting parents with kind words can make their day (even year). Your respect as a child can provide a level of satisfaction and contentment that you will only understand when you have your own kids.

When you respect your parents, you make living around them much easier. Does this mean life is perfect? No! Are you likely to argue or have different opinions? Yes! But living life together and experiencing the ups and downs of a normal family relationship should not change the underlying love for family.

Respect creates harmony in the family. Respect for all family members should exist in your family and extended family. In many ways that is the definition of family. It is not about self. Other family members are much easier to live with when there is an attitude of respect built on a foundation of humility.

Parents know things. Even though children grow up quickly, have access to tremendous amounts of information on the internet, and may even be considered smart, they do not have the vast experience of adults. Parents can teach children and young people amazing things if they have the opportunity. Parents know things because they experienced them.[14, 15]

"A child educated only at school is an uneducated child."

George Santayana

HONORING YOUR PARENTS

There are many ways one can show honor and respect to parents. Again, we are choosing brevity over extended discussion. It is relatively easy to understand these concepts and suggestions without extensive explanation.

It is interesting to recognize that many of the actions suggested to honor parents involve speech. Therefore we have grouped those all at the beginning of the list.

<u>GUARD YOUR SPEECH</u>

1. Always know they love you. It doesn't really matter how emotional, angry, or invested they may be about something, that will never impact the fact that they love you – even if you hurt them. Even if they are not affectionate or kindly to you or your position, that will not change the inherent nature of their love for you, even if they say it does in the heat of an argument.

2. Be thankful and grateful for what they do for you. Have an attitude of gratitude whether it is for the help of your parents or the gift of life. Don't take things for granted and be appreciative of what you receive and experience. There are many seasons in a life well lived. Always be grateful for what your parents provided and gave you. I am sure that some of you reading this paragraph did not have the family support you deserved. Rather than allowing bitterness to drive your life because of what you missed, make the most of your present circumstances.

3. Don't ignore parents. Talk to them regularly. If your parents are present, regardless of the circumstances, don't act as if they don’t exist. Introduce them to friends, include them in conversations, and ask them to participate in group activities. If you are alone with them, don't have your head in your electronics. Make the most of your time when you have the opportunity to be with them.

It is not the total amount of time that is important but the fact that it occurs on some regular basis. It does not have to be constant or extensive. It simply needs to be frequent enough that both the parent and child know what is happening in the life of the other. The child needs to be keenly aware of possible health problems as the parent ages.

4. Gentle speech is appreciated. Be very careful how you speak to parents. Harsh words, loud speech, or aggressive mannerisms can be very off-putting and in some cases even bring back unpleasant memories of child-raising. Do not act as if you are bossing them. Watch your tone and be kind and courteous.

Most adults do not like cursing, foul, or harsh language. If you or your parents speak using foul language it can often prevent any real communication. Gentle, calm, and courteous speech is far more effective than unnecessarily brutal words that rob you of normal conversations. Understanding is difficult to achieve when every other word is harsh or severe.

5. Courtesy will win the day, so be polite. The opposite of harsh speech is that which is laced with kindness and courtesy. If you are not used to, or have not been taught to say, "please" and "thank you," make it a priority in your life to learn to use them regularly. Do not cut others off when they are speaking. Do not ignore parents when they are responding to your questions. Don't butt in and change the subject before they have finished.

6. Visit regularly. If you live away from your parents, make sure to visit periodically. The lifestyle of the parent will dictate how often a visit is needed. If health is an issue, more frequent visits may be appropriate.

7. Don't talk back or be rude. This does not mean you necessarily agree with parents. You simply are not rude or aggressive about your feelings on issues. Remember, children and parents come from different generations and what was acceptable in one generation may not be acceptable to another. Important issues or questions should be discussed in a gentle and respectful manner. An argument accomplishes nothing.

8. Say, "I'm sorry" when appropriate. If there are misunderstandings between parents and children don't allow them to linger. Be humble and say, "I'm sorry," regardless if you are the parent or the child. Apologize when necessary. Do not allow the sun to go down on silly misunderstandings or differences of opinion that have no eternal value.

9. Don't ever lie. You should have learned this as a child. But lying to anyone, including parents, can only end in embarrassment, disappointment, or conflict. Do not lie in order to protect them. Do not lie to avoid disappointing them. Simply, do not lie. If you have a problem, trust your parents enough to share your situation. If you try to hide it or lie about it you will ultimately be found out and have accomplished nothing with your lies.

10. Listen to them. Listen to parents whether it is about something important or trivial. Normally they will give you advice they think will be best for you. If you want more input you may need to ask for it. But listening to parents does not mean that you follow their advice.

11. Do not grumble and complain. Avoid being a whiner or complainer. No one likes or appreciates a negative person who hates everything. If you grumble and complain about things, you will not be asked for your opinion or help on very many occasions. If you are asked to help out, do it with gladness.

12. Respect their wishes. You certainly should voice your concerns if you think parents are making a serious mistake, but you should not be belligerent. There will always be things you may not agree with, but in most cases you are only an advisor. Your only responsibility as a child is to warn them or give them your opinion.

13. Introduce your friends to them. Parents love to know about your friends. When you introduce your friends say something kind to them about your parents. Show your parents the special kindness of bragging on them. Include them whenever it is possible. Invite them even if all they will do is sit and observe.

15. Show pride. Exhibit pride in your parents to others when they are present. Honor them regardless of their financial position, academic achievement, or any other ability or social standing. Give your parents the respect and honor they deserve because they are your parents and you love them. Even if they are difficult parents, show them respect in the presence of others.

15. Do not create trouble. Be sensitive to the feelings and emotions of parents. They do care about you and will worry about you until the day you die – no matter what. That's their responsibility. There is nothing to be gained by pushing at sore spots. If a parent has a certain area of concern, try to be conscious of that in your speech and actions. If you are going bungee jumping, they don't need to know. If they do not like to fly, drive your car if possible.

If they can’t eat certain foods, make sure you have other foods they can eat. The bottom line is not to unnecessarily create problems that can be easily avoided.

16. Do not enjoy their mistakes. There is nothing that is likely to create a slow burn more than laughing at parent's mistakes or when they are embarrassed. It is not really wise to make fun of parents, even when they might deserve it. Everyone, including you, makes mistakes. Don't create a fire where ignoring the smoke will allow a small burn to be quickly forgotten.

<u>ALL OTHER</u>

17. Try to understand your parents' perspective. Parents and children will not necessarily think the same way about issues or problems. Take the time to consider how your parents will think about things. Remember, they will probably have a much different perspective because they have knowledge and experiences that you do not.

18. Serve their needs. Help them in any way possible during their adult and particularly advanced years. Be patient. You will never be able to repay them for their years of sacrifice, but you can signal that you recognize their position and status and that you are grateful.

19. Help them with work around the house. You can do this when you are age ten and for the rest of your life. There are times when your help will not be needed. Don't insist. There will be times when your help will be a blessing. Even your company or presence while working at some chore can be appreciated.

Children must understand that the aging process slows down the desire and motivation to do even normal or easy tasks. Plan a day when you are going to show up to help with chores.

20. Don't forget special occasions. Even if you visit regularly don't forget birthdays or anniversaries. Christmas, Thanksgiving Day, Valentine's Day, The Fourth of July, all can have special meaning to some parents. Your lifestyle and history of celebrating special days should dictate what you do.

21. Patience may be necessary. You will never know how patient your parents had to be with you when you were a baby or toddler – maybe even a teenager. You may not have had a tantrum in a public setting, but some children did. Return their past kindness with patience when it is needed.

22. Hug them. Touch is a powerful tool. It can send a message to the heart while speech only reaches the brain. Do not shy away from expressing your love and concern for your parents. If you were a kissing family, don't stop just because you are older. The power of touch can be the key to opening wonderful childhood memories.

23. Don't be tardy. It's like your days of going to school. If you promise or are expected to visit or call on Monday morning at 10:00 a.m., then make sure you are on schedule. As my wife used to say to our children, "There better be blood involved" if you're late! Everyone has busy schedules and yes things can come up at the last minute. If they do, call, text, or have someone get them a message that you will be late.

24. Watch your body language. Do not cross your arms when talking to parents or children. Do not do the gaze in the sky thing. Do not ignore what the other one is saying.

Don’t act defiant. Nothing is accomplished with unkind body posturing.

25. Obey the rules. Obey the house rules whether you are living with your parents or not. If they do not wear shoes in the house then you should comply with that practice. Respect and honor their space (home) as if it is a sacred place. Don't disrespect them because you ignore their lifestyle – even if you disagree. As a young child you have the responsibility and obligation to live under the rules of your parents. After you are out of the house you have the right to live anyway you wish, until you return and enter their home.

26. Respect their opinions, decisions, and core values. You do not have to agree with your parents' ideas or opinions, but don’t embarrass them or try to force your opinions or values on them. Respect the principles and core values they hold. Do not force what you think is right on them. You may, in fact, be wrong.

However, if you think your parents are being swindled or taken advantage of, do not be passive and hold back. You may need to recruit professional help to convince them of the truth and facts in a situation. Yes, there may be times you should allow them to make their own decisions – that is different than when someone is trying to cheat or steal from your parents.

27. Compromise, if necessary. It’s okay not to agree with parents. You should not expect to agree with everything they say or do. If you cannot agree it may be necessary to compromise. Compromise can be a good solution for many situations unless someone must violate their core values. If you cannot find common ground acceptable to both of you, compromise can be an ideal solution. You both give a little and allow life to continue.

28. Do not favor one parent. Favoring one parent over the other can lead to nothing but trouble. Big trouble! Sometimes it can seem impossible not to favor one parent over another but you are tempting fate if you think that is the best solution. Treating parents fairly does not necessarily mean you treat them the same.

29. Honor their interests. Parents have different likes and dislikes. They have different strengths and weaknesses. It is not in your best interest to treat their weaknesses the same as their strengths. Respect their skills and abilities and play to their strengths. You cannot act as if their interests, hobbies, and activities are not important to them. Your schedule and requests for help may need to account for their activities. Don't ask your Mom to babysit on days she is with her quilting friends. Don't ask your Dad to help with a project at your home on the day he plays golf with his friends. Obviously one day or one occurrence is not an issue, but creating a regular conflict exhibits the attitude that you don't care.

30. Go to lunch or dinner. Take them out to eat and catch up with everything they are doing. Be alert for problems they may have that they don't want to talk about because they don't want to bother you. If things are great, enjoy the food and company.[16, 17, 18]

"Children who are respected learn respect. Children who are cared for learn to care for those weaker than themselves."
Alice Miller

OBEDIENCE IS IMPORTANT FOR CHILDREN

How important is obedience? Must children always obey parents? Why should parents demand obedience? What happens in a home where obedience is not enforced? How important is the personal independence of children? Do children have rights and can they or should they refuse to obey? Who is really in charge? Do any of these questions ring a bell with you? Are you confused as to your rights, responsibility, authority, or ability to be a good parent or a responsible child?

All the issues and questions on this subject come down to the fundamental question, "Should parents insist that young children living at home obey their rules and boundaries?" It seems logical and obvious to me that there is only one possible answer to this question: "Yes." Unless the state is going to take on the responsibility of raising children, the responsibility for teaching and training children is clearly the responsibility of the parents. Do some parents do a poor job or do some parents even refuse to establish guidelines? Yes! But that does not change the legal and moral responsibility of the parents to set rules for children living in the home to obey. In my opinion any arguments to the contrary are absurd.

To allow children to make up their own rules or choose to obey only when they want to, is absurd and will lead to chaos and disharmony. Parents are called to love their children and train them to do what is right. If that does not occur, then peace and contentment cannot be established in the family or the community.

The new independent child

A logical question that arises from the relationship of child and parent is, "What happens when the child is an adult?"

When does an adult child become independent and is no longer under the control and responsibility of the parents?

This varies by country, culture, and circumstances. For most children it is when they are considered an adult. That may be defined by religion, culture, society, or laws. In the United States the legal age definition is generally considered 18. Culture, maturity, and family situations will impact the actual time of emancipation.

The relationship between child and parent changes when "adult" status is achieved. The child often leaves home, moves to another city, or assumes the responsibility of provision and protection for themselves. If the adult child does not leave home, they do not practically acquire all the normal responsibilities of an adult because they must still be governed by certain "rules of the house."

After the child is an adult, the relationship between family members must take into account the independence and new responsibilities of the adult child. Parents must now ask for favor or cooperation – they cannot demand it. For example, parents may strongly desire that a child come to "Sunday Dinner." But that is a request that is totally in the hands of the child. Deciding not to come to dinner or participate in the desired activities of parents should be decided by the child and the resulting decisions often have very little to do with whether the child loves the parent.

The transition from child to adult can be easy or difficult and everything in between for both the ascending child and the existing parents. Sometimes it can occur without any fanfare or discussion. But depending on your family circumstances and the relationship between family members it may require something special. A discussion may be needed, a celebration of the right-of-passage may be appropriate, or the event might occur naturally and with little fanfare.

It can be very helpful to have a discussion about mutual expectations and desires of both the parents and the child. It may be necessary to redefine the roles of everyone involved. For example, if the child is remaining in the parent's home, is there a curfew? What are the new house rules now that the child is an adult? What about finances, like rent and food? What does the adult child contribute to the household chores and responsibilities?

The home is the "domain" of the parents and they have the right to set certain rules. Hopefully they do not treat the adult child like a teenager. Rules should be reasonable and recognize the changing relationship. This is not a struggle for control of the household. If the child cannot live with the rules, they have the option to live elsewhere.

WHAT IS OBEDIENCE FOR YOUNG CHILDREN?

Modern generations often have a much different view of obedience than families 50 years ago. Unfortunately, some parents have even abdicated their parenting responsibilities and have allowed others to define for them what is fair, right, or appropriate in raising children. Today requiring a child's obedience might be considered an unreasonable requirement in some circles. Does that sound scary? It is!

What does true or real obedience mean? We are going to suggest three questions that inherently describe the nature of the obedience we think is appropriate.

1. WHEN IS OBEDIENCE REQUIRED: ***immediately*** (directly, instantly, promptly, right away)

A child who obeys when he want to is not being obedient. The behavior becomes rebellion. What's the child's attitude and how long does it take to comply? If it takes 10 minutes then it can be a day and you certainly would not think doing something 24 hours later constituted obedience. Obviously, if some request is understood to be done anytime today, then anytime today is acceptable.

Remember parents, you are teaching children the meaning of "prompt" in responding to those in authority. Don't be unreasonable, but do not allow stalling, acting as if you weren't heard, or obvious signs that they will get around to it on their own time. It should be understood you want something done now, unless you specify otherwise.

2. WHAT CONSTITUTES OBEDIENCE: ***doing it correctly*** (appropriately, properly, suitably)

When a child is told to do something specific, like take the garbage out, doing some other chore instead is not obedience. Taking it to the back door is not obedience. Mowing only 90% of the lawn is not obedience. Cleaning only certain parts of the bedroom is not obedience. Children must do the work properly and as everyone expects or it is rebellion.

3. HOW SHOULD INSTRUCTION BE ACCEPTED: ***pleasantly*** (agreeably, pleasingly)

Grumbling, complaining, temper tantrums, delaying, yelling, or any other form of unpleasant behavior is unacceptable. Do not allow a show of defiance or disrespect, no matter what it is. If the child is "obeying" promptly, doing the work properly, but exhibiting a rebellious or defiant attitude, they are not only disobedient but also disrespectful. They are not honoring your role as the parent. Children who act as if they are weary, tired, and resentful of your requests may need more work and chores until they learn how to act properly.[19]

"Children have to be educated, but they have also to be left to educate themselves."
Ernest Dimnet

CONCLUSION

Parents are just like everyone else: they make mistakes and they have feelings and desires just as we all do. If you think they made a mistake, talk with them about it. Communication with parents is extremely important. Parents cannot read minds, although there were times in my own childhood that I thought they could. As parents age it becomes more difficult for them to perceive what children are thinking.

If you are having difficulty with a parent, put yourself in their shoes before you do or say something you will regret. Depending on their age and experience, understanding the current generation and some of the new language and words may leave them in the dark. They may not even know what you are talking about and they sure don't want you to know they are clueless.

If your parents make a mistake, overreach, offend you, or even ignore you, they are still your parents. Take a deep breath and remember they will always be your parents, even if you are going through a tough time with them now. Regardless of the situation or who is at fault your goal must be to reconcile. Having an ongoing "fight" with parents or in-laws accomplishes very little and can have long lasting impact if things are said or done that are particularly insensitive.

Keep your eyes on the future and what you want to achieve and where you want the relationship to be in the future. Let the past fade away. Normally, if they understand they have hurt or wronged you, they will be sorry and seek to heal the situation. Again, communicate! And in difficult situations, your tone of voice and body language can be very helpful or hurtful. A hug accomplishes much more than a scowl. A touch on the shoulder can say more than your words. Parents will normally respond to heartfelt words of reconciliation.

Parenting is not easy whether it is your parenting or the parenting of your parents. It can be very difficult depending on circumstances. Parents and children have an inherent bond and a heart desire to connect. The family bond is unique and can always be restored with love, understanding, kindness, and forgiveness.

Love will always win over hate. Kindness will always win over getting even. Forgiveness will always be better than estrangement.

Wisdom to Action Challenge

Think about recent advice your parents have given you. Even if you disagree, take the time to genuinely consider their perspective. Identify one piece of advice you will reflect on this week, and assess how it might benefit your life, even if you ultimately choose a different path.

Chapter 8
Tips for a Happier Family

"Having children makes you no more a parent than having a piano makes you a pianist."
Michael Levine

GENERAL

Obeying parents is one of the most difficult things to do whether you are a toddler, teenager, or adult child living at home. The issues causing conflict can be fairness, independence, or anything that causes children and parents to be at odds. For most of us, parents offer advice or instruction out of genuine and sincere care, children are well served to listen and evaluate what they have to say. Parents come from a different generation and it may be hard to understand their reasoning, but we should not reject their advice out of hand.

Parents may be trying to navigate the change from parenting a helpless child to a confident teenager, or to a fully independent adult. Both may be struggling with dramatic changes in their lives. Calm and patience can prevent hard feelings. Children do need more freedom and they must be recognized for their abilities, but they must also be protected from themselves. The transition can be a time of stress that is best navigated with love and respect.

Communication is always the key, whether you are asking for permission or seeking forgiveness. Teenagers who want to stretch the existing rules should not wait until ten minutes before a deadline to ask for rules to be lifted or changed. If there are reasons for the failure, or extenuating circumstances, explain the situation. Respectful communication can solve many problems.

"Each day of our lives we make deposits in the memory banks of our children."
Charles R. Swindoll

TIPS FOR A HAPPY FAMILY

Family harmony. Family members must appreciate and look out for each other. They must protect each other. Nothing is gained by family members acting as if they have some higher position or advantage in the home. Parents should work hard at creating and maintaining good relationships between siblings. Family members should appreciate each other and know how comforting it is to be in a loving family environment. Many children do not have that opportunity.

But children frequently try to test the boundaries and limits to see what they can get away with. Where can they gain some advantage? Boundaries are necessary because children are inherently bad. They must be taught what is right and the difference between good and bad. But boundaries must be reasonable and not overwhelming.

Make it a rule that you will respect each other and treat each other as family. That means you will protect and provide for each other. The ideal is that whenever anyone comes home, those in the house are happy to see them. Because you are family, you like each other, no matter how much competitive give and take occurs among particular family members.

Spend time together. Do things as a family. Pay attention to how other members in the family are doing. Have a home atmosphere that causes your children to want to invite their friends. Create memories! Fight boredom and inactivity. Children or adults should not be spending their time alone away from others staring at a TV or other electronics.

Simply do things together. Attend classes together, whether it is art, cooking, or home repair. Maybe learn to dance! Share the same hobbies if appropriate. Simply have fun together. It doesn't really matter how skilled you become. It can even be fun to be the worst at something.

Have specified times when the family will participate in fun, learning, or skill building activities. If possible, go on vacations together. If you cannot eat together, try to have another activity each day where the entire family is present. Maybe it's homework. Maybe it's a bedtime story. Maybe it's a game. Having a good time with family is infinitely valuable.

When parents come home, the kids should be the first priority for some period of time. That child may have been waiting at the window for the parent to come home and they will be devastated if ignored when the parent comes home.

Family stories. Children who know the stories of their parents and siblings tend to have greater bond with each other. Activities and teaching moments should be such that they reside in the memories of children. Parents can create knowledge and appreciation of family by telling stories about family at the dinner table. Children who know about family tend to have a stronger sense of identity as a family. Stories can be fun or instructive. They can also teach about life. Life was not always easy for great-grandmother, but she persevered . . . .

Marriage is sacred. The relationship of the parents and the marriage must be recognized as sacred. It is vital to protect the children, but they do not come first. The marriage comes first and together the parents raise the family. I remember having to tell one of my teenage children that her mother came first in my life and if she (the daughter) wanted to remain in my good graces she had better get her act together because if she was going to force me to make a choice, I was choosing her mother.

Parents cannot allow children to become so important that they destroy the marriage. Parents must make time for children, but children must allow time for parents to have time together. If the marriage is not honored, then the relationship with children will ultimately be compromised.

Argue in private. Never have "fights" in front of the kids. Even normal discussions can be misinterpreted by younger children. While some disagreement and frustration is inevitable, don't make it a habit to hash out all your differences in front of the family.

Eat together. Have you ever heard the cliché, "Families that eat together, stay together." It's more true than you may think. A lot can happen at the dinner table. The dinner table can be a time of teaching and learning. It can sometimes be a time to catch up. If you cannot eat together every night, then try for as many nights per week as schedules permit.

Family first. Family comes before friends and work. Both parents and children must prioritize family time and activities. It is not fair or appropriate if the only ones making it a priority are the children. Life cannot be operated as if it is some kind of academic regimen. If kids get bored they may start looking for excitement elsewhere. That will usually be outside the house and there will be no supervision.

Don't allow work to keep you away from family. If your family is not a priority in your lives it will be difficult to maintain a marriage or raise a family. Don't think that your spouse and children don't know your priorities! Continuous failure to be present with the family sends a clear message that you don't really care.

It's not always easy to balance home life with a challenging and demanding job. In some cases that may mean you have to decide between one or the other. But a family cannot always be in last place on your priority list. Workaholics can lose their family if they cannot find an acceptable way to balance their work and family. If work always comes first, serious damage will be done to desired relationships that are inherently more important than the work. Most career oriented professionals can find a way to fit family goals into their career objectives if they want to. Wise choices and priorities can assure that both the family and the career are successful.

Respect other family members. As a parent you want your children to respect others. They must be taught to respect and appreciate their siblings and other people. Some parents think this will happen automatically because it is the family or a friend. Children don't necessarily think that way unless you set an example, talk about the importance of family, and model the same behavior you want followed. Love and respect do not happen automatically. They must be taught and earned.

Have reasonable after-school activities. It can be easy to over-schedule school activities. Parents can become "personal drivers" for both their kids and others in the neighborhood. Some parents say their children are never home at the same time and meals cannot be taken together because of the hectic schedules. This all occurs because of the decisions you make as a family. Not every child has to be in sports, dance class, band, or learn a second language. Moderation and balance is the ideal.

Family rituals. Family rituals can be helpful in building expectations, history, and relationships, but they are not absolutely necessary. If rituals exist they should have flexible timeframes. You don't have to eat pizza every Friday night. Family rituals can bring families together and create special bonds and memories. They should not necessarily last for a lifetime. We always baked cookies on the first day of school. Other families make pancakes on Saturday mornings. Maybe you go sledding on a special hill at the first snow. It doesn't really matter what you do if it has meaning to your family and does not become overly controlling on your life. For example, your Christmas rituals must be modified when children leave the home, and particularly when they have their own families.

Yelling is a bad habit. Yelling at a child may be necessary on occasion but it should not be a common occurrence. Children who yell and scream at each other are not appealing. Yelling is either a sign of a lack of self-control or a bad habit.

Be flexible. Flexibility does not mean you do not enforce the rules and boundaries. But they do change under different circumstances. They change with the age and maturity of the children. They change when they are not effective. And the entire relationship changes when children leave home, get married, or become adults. Rules and boundaries must change when circumstances change.

There must be time alone, if needed. Some people, particularly less social humans, need time to be by themselves. It's not that they dislike the people around them, they simply need some quiet time with less hustle and bustle. They need time to breathe! It's in their DNA!

Adults have the advantage of the other parent when they need some down time. Mom often needs time just to get away from the noise. Children can drain the life out of you if you don't have time for refreshment from time-to-time. Alone time doesn't make you a bad parent or bad spouse. Most people need it. Finding such times can refresh the spirit in many ways.

But rest and refreshment is important for everyone in the family, not just adults. Children have different personalities and temperaments. Some of them need more alone or quiet times compared to their siblings. Don't fall into the mistake of forcing constant togetherness on everyone.

Reduce stress. Children don't need to be stressed out and they don't want their parents tired and stressed. If you think they don't see and feel your stress, just ask them. Family stress can cause learning difficulties, health problems, obedience issues, eating disorders, etc.

Here are some simple suggestions for reducing stress:

- Don't worry about work problems when you're at home and home problems when you're at work.
- Know what is expected at work so stress reduced.
- Work overtime only under limited circumstances.
- Focus on positive outcomes, not problems.
- Art and music are great for reducing anxiety.
- Alcohol is never a good solution.
- Watch funny videos or something humorous.
- Keep a diary of your thoughts, concerns, and goals.
- Stop bad habits you may have acquired.
- Remind yourself that worry solves nothing, the worst is not likely to happen.
- Give yourself a pep-talk.

- Spend time with good friends.
- Help somebody else. Give your time to others, particularly those in need.
- Have a daily quiet time. Meditate or pray.
- Participate in a favorite hobby or sport.
- Spend time outdoors. Take a walk.
- Do some light chores around the house.
- Eat cookies or do something else athletic. ☺

No unnecessary competition. Don't make every activity or outing into some kind of competition. It's not healthy. Competitive activities are fine but unless the activity naturally a competition, don't make it into one. There should be no winners or losers in normal family activities. There should be no competition to see who cleans their room the quickest or the best. And never compare one child to another.

Be part of a larger community. Families that are apart of other groups have a big advantage over those trying to bring up their family alone. The group may be an extended family network, a religious community, or a small friends group. Usually a larger group like 10-15 people is a better and more effective "community."

Have the proper mindset about discipline. Rather than thinking discipline is a punishment, it is much better to think of it as a way of teaching and training your children how to survive. They must learn how to survive and be successful in an environment that does not want to cooperate. They need to learn how to live and thrive in an environment that can be harsh and demanding.

Self-discipline is often the key. Being in control and having knowledge of what you need to do and accomplish is very important. You will often be faced with alternatives, some of which you may desire but are not good for you or your children. You must be strong enough to say no. Don't allow yourself to blame your poor decisions on others, particularly your children.[20, 21, 22]

"One father is more than a hundred schoolmasters."
George Herbert

CONCLUSION

There are many things you can do as parents to encourage the proper development of children. Any kind of hands-off policy will leave understanding and growth to chance and time. That will usually produce great disappointment for you and be of little benefit to your children.

You should decide when you will be proactive in teaching concepts and when you want children to learn on their own. Your children and their personalities must dictate what you do and when you do it. Flexibility is very important. You must take the time to think about and consider each child and determine what is likely to be effective and what is not. Often trial and error is the only real alternative.

Don't allow insecurities, egos, or bullies to operate in your home. Think of all the bad types of behavior you can imagine and do not let them get a foothold in your family. If you have a bad situation developing, you will know it, so don't ignore it. The longer it continues, the more difficult it will be to get it resolved. Don't hope or assume it will go away. Put a stop to it immediately!

Be kind and loving but exercise your position and wisdom as a parent. Stop inappropriate language or behavior. When someone needs to be the adult, stand up and be counted. Unacceptable and inappropriate behavior that is allowed to continue, fester, and become acceptable can destroy a family.

There are many obvious behaviors that you should not tolerate: neglect, physical or verbal abuse, dishonesty, favoritism, secrecy, oppression, bullying, pampering, etc. These behaviors can exist in the children, in-laws, grandparents, and other caregivers, including the spouse.

It does not really matter the source of the problem, an intelligent and loving parent cannot allow destructive behavior, no matter where it is coming from. If you allow the insecurities of someone in your family or extended family to cause hurtful behavior, your children will observe that you allowed it and perceive it is acceptable. If it is bad behavior, it should not be allowed to impact your family, no matter what!

"Feelings of worth can flourish only in an atmosphere where individual differences are appreciated, mistakes are tolerated, communication is open, and rules are flexible – the kind of atmosphere that is found in a nurturing family."
Virginia Satir

Wisdom to Action Challenge

Identify one area where you can cultivate more respect and appreciation within your family. Take specific actions to prioritize personal growth, practice forgiveness, and let go of grudges this week, observing how these efforts enhance your family's overall happiness and well-being.

Chapter 9
My Family Plan

To repeat what we said earlier about your "Love Plan," in the Life Planning Series we have typically provided a substantial outline to develop a plan of action for the given subject. We will not provide that extensive process in this book. If you want to do a more extensive plan, we recommend picking up a copy of *CHOOSE Integrity* or the *Life Planning Handbook*. Each of the "Choose" books in the Series contains a more extensive planning process and you can adapt that to what you want to accomplish for your "Love" or "*Family*" objectives or plan.

In this section we will provide an abbreviated planning approach to improving your family life skills. There are five major areas you might want to address as it pertains to the family topics we have discussed:

PARENTS:
1. Improving parenting skills.
2. Parents disciplining children.

CHILDREN:
3. Children honoring parents.
4. Children obeying parents.

FAMILY:
5. Improving the family atmosphere and dynamic.

PLANNING OUTLINE

The following outline is provided for addressing any subject or area that you want to work on whether the perspective is as a parent, child, or family member. Use this outline for any of the areas you want to improve or develop. We suggest that you begin with one subject at a time, or several if they are closely related. Before you begin we suggest that you review the sections in this book that are of particular interest and make notes on issues, questions, or possible actions. Then complete the following:

1. Statement of the challenge, issue, problem, or subject:

____

2. Statement of your goal or objective (brief and concise):

____

3. List *all reasonable* actions you might take to achieve your goal.

a. ____________________
b. ____________________
c. ____________________
d. ____________________
e. ____________________
f. ____________________

4. List the two best action steps in priority order:

a. ____________________
b. ____________________

5. Do one or both until you have made some progress and then choose another action step, or change to a new subject.

Appendix A
Parenting Styles

GENERAL

Parenting styles are not a particular focus for this book. It is not our goal to identify, teach, or train the reader in any particular parenting style. But over the years a great deal has been written about parenting styles. Therefore, we are including this information for those of you who would like an overview of the different parenting styles.

Experts in the field have generally tried to group these styles into various categories. It is not our intent here to go into great depth or try to present an all-inclusive overview of parenting styles. If you would like to have a general understanding of different styles of parenting, hopefully you find this Appendix helpful.

Determining which style is right for your family should be a personal choice based on your temperament, your child's temperament, and your family's discipline philosophies. There isn't a single type of parenting style or discipline that will work for all kids or all families. It's likely that you must take a somewhat broad approach, where you use techniques from various types of discipline strategies that best fit your needs.

Parenting styles are simply the ways or concepts parents use to train children. Parents want to produce a desired behavior from their child. It is those practices that are referred to as parenting styles. At one end of the process the parent encourages (even demands) a certain behavior and at the other end the child responds in some way. It is the different approaches to trying to elicit the desired response that defines the different styles that we will outline in this Appendix.

Why have different parenting styles?

There are many effective techniques, practices, or aspects that a parent could use in interacting with their children. For example, how do you support, control, approve, monitor, interact, punish, or reward your child? Parents frequently have different parenting styles depending on the child's gender. But it's not really because of the gender, it's really because of the nature and personality of the child. A child who is more emotional or very quiet and reserved will require a different parenting style than a child who is very active and rough, and who insists on being "in charge."

NOTE: There are two styles with similar names but different approaches to parenting. We have listed these at the beginning. While both styles have strict elements, authoritative parents balance rules with nurturing, fostering a healthier environment for their children's growth and development. The authoritarian approach is much more demanding.

AUTHORITATIVE STYLE

It is believed this style is the most frequently used by parents because many believe it is the one that most consistently produces the desired outcomes. It is often considered the ideal style because it includes warmth and flexibility. Boundary-based styles focus on making the rules and boundaries clear upfront. Children are then given choices and understand clearly the consequences for misbehavior. The desired result is that children know what is expected and develop good emotional and social skills that result in high achievement.

In authoritative parenting children are told what to do. There is typically no negotiation and obedience is taught. House chores are often assigned and the rules and boundaries make logical sense. Parents are warm and responsive to a child's physical and emotional needs.

The advantages of authoritative parenting are that children gain high self-esteem and confidence allowing them to have assertive personalities. Good emotional control is present producing good academic performance. The children typically have well-developed social skills.

Instead of saying, "Eat your vegetables because I told you so!" an authoritative parent would generally say, "Eat your vegetables because they'll help you grow strong and healthy." If a child grabs his friend's toy, an authoritative parent might say, "I understand that you also want to play with this truck. However, your friend is playing with that toy right now. You can play with this toy until he is ready to give you a turn with the truck.

If the child is hungry, rather than letting the child eat anything and everything, an authoritative parent would say, "You may have a piece of cheese or an apple. Which would you prefer?"

POSITIVE STYLE

Positive parenting overlaps significantly with authoritative parenting and is described as positive guidance and support. The primary objective is to encourage children and to identify the middle ground or situation where both parent and child can be comfortable. Positive discipline is based on praise and encouragement. Parents teach problem-solving skills and work with their children to develop solutions. Positive discipline uses family meetings and an authoritative approach to addressing behavior issues.

There are established guidelines and coaching to comply with the rules. Positive parents don't teach do's and don'ts, or impose strict rules. They are very supportive of the child and allow him to figure out a solution with guidance from the parents. The strategy is to avoid power struggle between the parent and child.

For example, if a child is taking a long time to get ready and you're running late, instead of saying "Hurry up! We're late!" a positive parent would say, "Would you rather put on your shoes or your jacket first?"

AUTHORITARIAN (Strict)

This style demands a lot and often has a low response (warmth) when the desired behavior is achieved. This style places a very high value on the virtue of obedience. Rules are rigorously enforced. The goal is that children are well-behaved. This style can cause children to struggle with independence and sometimes decision-making.

An authoritarian parent demands obedience. The child's viewpoint is not considered and there is never any negotiation. What the parent demands is what is expected. The standards are generally very high.

The problems this style creates is that children are prone to feel low self-esteem and there may be a lack of trust. The style is typically not open to experimentation with new ideas: "What I say goes." Therefore children don't learn to take responsibility.

For example, if a child broke a toy by accident, the parent may decide to ground the child for a week due to the child's carelessness. If the child requests a snack, the parent will often say no because that would violate the one-snack rule.

UNINVOLVED STYLE

Some people describe this style as neglectful. It ranks very low on the scale of requiring what the parent requests or demands. It generally is very low on emotional involvement between parent and child. Uninvolved parents provide minimal guidance, attention, and support to their children. They may be indifferent or overwhelmed, leading to a lack of responsiveness and little nurturing. As a result, children often struggle with emotions, self-esteem, and total well-being.

Neglectful parenting can often fail to meet the physical and emotional needs of the child. This can include food, exercise, companionship, etc. the parent is often totally disengaged from the child and any relationship is emotional and physically distant.

Often the child must learn to provide for themselves. They may fear dependency on other people, and they are typically emotionally withdrawn and distant.

If a child grabs their friend's toy, the neglectful parent makes no attempt to intervene, rationalize, or correct the behavior. When the child wants a snack, the parent wouldn't offer a healthy snack. In some serious cases, the neglectful parent might not respond to their child's hunger at all.

PERMISSIVE STYLE

With this parenting style there is a low demand for correct behavior. Permissive parents generally try to be friends with their children and rather than tell them what to do, they will ask them if they want to do something. This parenting style is characterized by leniency and low demands. Permissive parents are indulgent and avoid setting strict rules. They prioritize their child's happiness and freedom over discipline. Consequently, children raised in permissive households may struggle with self-control and boundaries.

In a permissive parenting environment there are few behavioral expectations and little discipline. The hope is to avoid conflicts and encourage harmony. The parent will often try to encourage equality between themselves and the child. This style does produce independent thinking, but bribery and praise are control techniques used to obtain obedience.

The impact on the children of permissive parenting is that they tend to act impulsively and often make poor decisions. Managing financial matters is not easy. The have fewer emotional skills and lower academic achievement is usually the result.

If a child a child grabs a toy from their friend, the permissive parent would choose not to intervene. If they want a snack, permissive parents would put no restrictions or limits on what or when the child can eat.

UNCONDITIONAL REGARD STYLE (Gentle)

The unconditional regard or gentle parenting style emphasizes empathy, unconditional love, and positive communication no matter what the circumstances.

Discipline often focuses on preventing problems. Kids are given consequences, but the gentle discipline isn't about instilling sorrow or shame for misbehavior. Instead, parents often use humor and distraction.

The focus of gentle discipline is parents managing their own emotions while addressing a child's misbehavior. Parents avoid punishments and instead focus on teaching through connection, mutual respect, and active listening. Children in this environment tend to develop strong self-esteem, emotional intelligence, and healthy relationships.

There is complete support for the child and parents love the child for who they are. They will ignore what they are not and don't do. If the child tells you that they accidentally broke your favorite dish, rather than be mad at the child, you respond with a comment such as, "That's okay. It's only a dish. Just be more careful next time."

NURTURING STYLE (Slow)

The nurturing or slow parenting style encourages parents to prioritize quality over quantity. Rather than overscheduling their children with organized activities, slow parenting allows kids to explore the world at their own pace. This is a style that helps children live without their parent's constant protection. Thus, the child develops their own interests and grows to be their own person. It emphasizes unhurried interactions, empathy, and meaningful connections.

Children raised in this style tend to develop a strong sense of self and a deeper understanding of the world. Thus parents style encourage more family time. The end goal is to enable the child to be satisfied with themselves.

Parents limit electronics or things that distract from real life situations. The children help organize and plan daily activities. Simpler toys that force the child to be more creative are utilized. When a child wants to watch TV, the parent encourages them to go outside to explore nature or read a book instead.

HELICOPTER STYLE

The term “helicopter parenting” was coined in “Parenting with Love and Logic: Teaching Children Responsibility” by Jim Fay and Foster W. Cline. Parents attempt to keep their children very close and under their control, often described as "hovering." These parents have a fear that they will lose control of their child. They distrust their children’s ability to take care of themselves and make decisions on their own. The child may have grown up, but they haven’t outgrown their parent’s micromanagement and hovering. A large issue with over-parenting is that kids aren’t able to develop the psychological resilience to endure the issues that develop when they are adults.

Helicopter parents have difficulty allowing their children to be over-engaged. They are constantly intervening – on behalf of their kids – and covering for the child’s mistakes. They will do school work or job applications for the child to make sure they are done correctly. There is constant contact with the child via technology.

There may be excessive praise and encouragement by the helicopter parent. Parental temper tantrums are even possible. These parents will call their college student in the morning to make sure they’re awake in time for class.

***"Where parents do too much for their children,
the children will not do much for themselves."***
Elbert Hubbard

THE MOST EFFECTIVE STYLE

The most effective or the best style to use is the one that works best for the particular child. Parenting styles can be cultural and depend on the child's temperament and personality. Whatever style is chosen the goal is to make sure there are normal harmonious family relationships, not control or domination of the child.

The child's personality is an important aspect to consider. Historically, parenting styles were chosen based on the natural inclination of the parent rather than the needs of the child. Today, parenting styles are more geared toward the child. Each child and parent will likely have a different way to interact with others. We are all different. Each parent has to find the best way to work with each child's individual personality and temperament.

Primary References For Appendix A

1 A complete guide to different types of parenting methods; Feb 15, 2018; by Anna Bohren; https://yourbrain.health/parenting-styles/
2 Fifteen Effective Parenting Skills Every Parent Should Know & Have; https://high5test.com/parenting-skills/
3 What Is Your Parenting Style, and Why Does It Matter? By Lauren Pardee; https://www.parents.com/parenting/better-parenting/style/parenting-styles-explained/
4 Parenting Styles, Wikipedia, https://en.wikipedia.org/wiki/Parenting_styles

Other Resources For Appendix A

<u>Books:</u>

--- "Parenting from the Inside Out: How a Deeper Self-Understanding Can Help You Raise Children Who Thrive" by Daniel J. Siegel and Mary Hartzell.
--- "The Whole-Brain Child: 12 Revolutionary Strategies to Nurture Your Child's Developing Mind" by Daniel J. Siegel and Tina Payne Bryson.
--- "How to Talk So Kids Will Listen & Listen So Kids Will Talk" by Adele Faber and Elaine Mazlish.
--- "Parenting with Love and Logic: Teaching Children Responsibility" by Foster Cline and Jim Fay.

<u>Internet:</u>

--- "The Psychology Behind Different Types of Parenting Styles" https://jessup.edu/blog/academic-success/the-psychology-behind-different-types-of-parenting-styles/
--- American Academy of Pediatrics (AAP): The AAP website provides articles and resources on parenting styles and child development.

Appendix B
Physical Discipline of Children

WHAT DOES THE BIBLE SAY?

NOTE: This information is provided for those who want to know what the Bible says about correction and particularly physical discipline. Remember that discipline is a general term meaning the process used to gain obedience or conformity to some standard of behavior. Punishment is a penalty for disobedience often implying suffering, pain, or loss. It should be noted that unnecessarily harsh physical correction or abuse is <u>never</u> acceptable. There are many punishments that would not be physical in nature or application that can be very effective.

DISCIPLINE – General

Proverbs 4:1-5 ***1 My children, listen when your father corrects you. Pay attention and learn good judgment, 2 for I am giving you good guidance. Don't turn away from my instructions. 3 For I, too, was once my father's son, tenderly loved as my mother's only child. 4 My father taught me, Take my words to heart. Follow my commands, and you will live. 5 Get wisdom; develop good judgment. Don't forget my words or turn away from them. (NLT)***

This proverb indicates that the parent is to discipline the child and the child is to listen. The instruction is to "take my words to heart" and follow my commands. The result will be the gaining of understanding and wisdom.

Proverbs 5:23 ***He will die for lack of self-control; he will be lost because of his great foolishness. (NLT)***

How can one die because of lack of discipline or self-control? Isn't that a bit extreme? Not necessarily. The problem identified here is the folly of great foolishness. It is given very high importance because it might produce serious consequences (death).

There are many dangers because one is foolish and lacks self-control. For example, driving while intoxicated, participating in an armed robbery, etc. The lack of self-discipline can cause one to be led astray and the consequence can be very great.

Proverbs 12:1 ***To learn, you must love discipline; it is stupid to hate correction. (NLT)***

Many of the real important life lessons are learned through discipline and correction (experience) rather than out of a book! Wisdom comes because of the serious plea and teaching of loving parents, other trusted advisors, or the observance of what happens to people who make poor decisions and suffer the consequences.

The strong language in the proverbs is for the one who hates (ignores or rejects) correction. They are often described as stupid because they lack understanding of the purpose of correction and discipline.

Proverbs 15:5 ***Only a fool despises a parent's discipline; whoever learns from correction is wise. (NLT)***
Proverbs 19:18 ***Discipline your children while there is hope. Otherwise you will ruin their lives. (NLT)***

Discipline is said to be the proper course of action in raising a child. There is hope in disciplining a child. Lack of discipline removes the hope and the alternative expectation is ruin, caused by the one who fails to discipline.

DISCIPLINE – The Rod

Proverbs 13:24 *Those who spare the rod of discipline hate their children. Those who love their children care enough to discipline them. (NLT)*

Does it make sense to say that a parent hates a child because they did not discipline them? On one level no, but the seriousness of not lovingly correcting and instructing a child (physically when necessary) borders on not loving the child. The fundamental responsibility of a parent is to train up a child. It is absolutely imperative that the parent teach the child what they need to know to survive in an evil world. If the parent refuses or does a poor job, the result can be devastating for the child.

Proverbs 22:15 *A youngster's heart is filled with foolishness, but physical discipline will drive it far away. (NLT)*

The terrible fact we learn from 22:15 is that the heart of a child is prone to foolishness. That probably does not surprise too many parents, but it may surprise many sons and daughters. Why would physical discipline be the suggested method of correction to destroy foolishness? There may be several reasons:

- Foolish behavior is very serious and is inherently present. It needs quick and decisive correction.

- Soft words will often not correct a serious problem for a child because they don't really understand the serious nature of what they are doing.

Proverbs 29:15, 17, 19 *To discipline a child produces wisdom, but a mother is disgraced by an undisciplined child. . . . 17 Discipline your children, and they will give you peace of mind and will make your heart glad. . . 19 Words alone will not discipline a servant; the words may be understood, but they are not heeded. (NLT)*

A youth who is "undisciplined" and allowed to make decisions without parental guidance is described here as a disgrace to the family. Many young people, typically teenagers, think they know more than their parents and they often believe they can make adult decisions. Some can but many cannot.

Verse 29:19 says that words alone will not accomplish the objective because a child does not get the message. The implication is that serious correction is necessary to get their attention. Proverbs 29:21 says, "*A servant pampered from childhood will become a rebel.*" *(NLT)* A servant here can represent anyone, including sons and daughters.

Wisdom to Action Challenge

Carefully consider the principles outlined in this appendix. How can you ensure that your discipline methods are rooted in love and responsibility, aimed at guiding your children away from foolishness and potential harm? Take time to reflect on the balance between discipline and fostering wisdom in your children's lives, ensuring they understand the consequences of their actions.

Transformation Roadmap

Wisdom That Transforms!

1. Love, in all its forms—romantic, platonic, familial—enhances emotional well-being, reduces stress and anxiety, fosters resilience, and contributes to longevity. It is essential for living a fulfilling and connected life by helping individuals feel understood and supported.

2. Acting with love aligns individuals with their deepest truth and authentic self, enabling personal growth and a sense of purpose. Love is both the source of profound joy and grief, but embracing it allows one to live meaningfully and in harmony with their core identity.

3. Acts of caring love, such as offering support and kindness, reduce stress, anxiety, and depression while boosting physical health through stronger immunity and better cardiovascular function.

4. By prioritizing kindness and selfless acts, caring love fosters deeper connections, gratitude, and a sense of fulfillment, enabling individuals to live with greater joy and meaning.

5. Building nurturing relationships through empathy and unconditional support fosters children's emotional resilience and well-being while creating a secure foundation for their growth and exploration.

6. Utilizing consistent routines, clear boundaries, and stress management techniques improves parent-child interactions, promotes mental wellness, and cultivates a stable, supportive home environment that benefits the entire family.

7. Discipline as guidance, not as punishment. Effective discipline focuses on teaching rather than punishing, using techniques like setting clear limits, logical consequences, and redirection to help children learn responsibility and self-control.

8. Consistently applying discipline helps children learn self-control and understand the consequences of their actions, offering them hope for a better future and preventing the potential ruin that can come from a lack of guidance.

9. Applying rules and consequences consistently, while reinforcing good behavior, strengthens the parent-child bond and creates a stable environment that supports both behavioral learning and healthy development.

10. Treating your parents with respect, appreciation, and provision, regardless of their past actions, reduces potential regrets and promotes inner peace.

11. Children, should listen and obey their parents. Listening to parents is a sign of appreciation and respect. Valuing and considering your parents' advice does not require you to act on all of their suggestions when you are no longer living in their home.

12. Cultivate respect and honor in your family. Treat your family members, especially parents, with honor and respect, valuing their guidance and support to foster stronger relationships and personal well-being. Strive to be the best version of yourself, which ultimately honors your family and enhances your life.

***Your decisions shape your life.
Start building with intention!***

Free PDF

MAKE WISE DECISIONS

[Get the ebook version for 99 cents]

Consequences Shape Lives.

This book discusses the nature of decisions and explores eight essential questions to make better decisions.

You are a few decisions away from transforming your life. You can make better decisions! This resource has sections on what makes a poor decision, questions to ask yourself, traps to avoid, short and sweet decisions, the wise decision framework, and twenty ways to be wise. It also has a handy decision-making checklist. (12 pages)

Free PDF: https://getwisdompublishing.com/resource-registration/

Kindle ebook for 99 cents: https://www.amazon.com/dp/B0FG8NC53J

Ebook

Free PDF

Ten Steps to Wise Choices

Timeless Wisdom. Practical Tools. Lasting Impact.

Free PDF

Life Improvement Principles

[Get the ebook version for 99 cents]

You can live your best life!

Welcome to a journey of discovery! In case you have forgotten, your actions have consequences. Unlock your potential! This book (60+ pages) provides the overview of all our strategies and wisdom principles to live your best life. You *can* transform your life! Get your wisdom-based roadmap to a better life and unlock all the possibilities for growth and success.

Free PDF: https://getwisdompublishing.com/resource-registration/

Kindle ebook for 99 cents:
https://www.amazon.com/dp/B0FG883KZM

Ebook

Free PDF

Make it your life goal to
be the best you can be!

Discover Wisdom and live the life you deserve.

Your Next Steps

Change Your Life with purpose and intention!

Should you read other books in this series?

We recommend that if you acquire any books in the Series, you should also obtain *CHOOSE Integrity*. This is the foundational book in the series. We also believe the four books covering the other Primary Life Principles would be particularly useful for living a better life: Friends, Speech, Diligence (Work), and Money.

CHOOSE Faith

This is a unique book in the Series. It addresses all the important spiritual type questions you might consider. It answers questions like: Does God exist? Why should I care about faith? What's religion all about? Does eternal life really exist? I don't know the right questions to ask. What is the truth? This book will help you find answers to your spiritual questions.

LIFE PLANNING HANDBOOK

This book is also unique. If you are interested in doing a complete life plan that covers all aspects of your life, not just a specific topic like those addressed in The Life Planning Series, go to:

https://www.amazon.com/dp/1952359325

You can live a better life.
Just Decide You Want to!

The Life Planning Series

These books can improve your life.

LIFE PLANNING HANDBOOK	**A Life Plan will shape your life journey!** The next step in your life planning.
CHOOSE INTEGRITY	**Life Principle:** Be honest, live with integrity, and base your life on truth.
CHOOSE FRIENDS WISELY	**Life Principle:** Choose your friends wisely.
CHOOSE THE RIGHT WORDS	**Life Principle:** Guard your speech.
CHOOSE GOOD WORK HABITS	**Life Principle:** Be diligent and a hard worker.
CHOOSE FINANCIAL RESPONSIBILITY	**Life Principle:** Make sound financial choices.

CHOOSE A POSITIVE SELF-IMAGE	**Life Principle:** Be confident in who you are.
CHOOSE LEADERSHIP	**Life Principle:** Lead well and be a loyal follower.
CHOOSE CORE VALUES	**Life Principle:** Core values will drive your life.
CHOOSE LOVE AND FAMILY	**Life Principle:** Build strong relationships.
CHOOSE FAITH	*Your Spiritual Guidebook for Questions about Religion, God, Heaven, Truth, Evil, and the Afterlife.*

Go to: **https://www.amazon.com/dp/B09TH9SYC4**
to get your copy.

Create a life based on purpose, meaning, and lasting fulfillment.

Acknowledgments

My wife has patiently persevered while I indulged my interest in this subject. Thank you for your patience.

Our older daughter has been an invaluable resource. She has also graciously produced our website at www.lifeplanningtools.com

Our middle daughter designed all the covers for this series. We are very grateful for her help, talent and creativity.

Notes

QUOTES – ACCURACY: We have used a number of quotes throughout this book that came from our files, notes, books, public articles, the Internet, etc. We have made no attempt to verify that these quotes were actually written or spoken by the person they are attributed to. Regardless of the source of these quotes, the wisdom of the underlying message is relative to the content in this book and worth noting, even if the source reference is erroneous.

QUOTES – SOURCE: Unless otherwise specifically footnoted below the quotes used herein can be sourced from a number of different websites on the Internet that provide lists of quotes by subject or author. The same or similar quotes will appear on multiple sites. The sources for the quotes used in this book include:

--azquotes.com
--everydaypower.com
--goodhousekeeping.com
--goodreads.com/quotes
--graciousquotes.com
--notable-quotes.com
--thoughtcatalog.com
--brainyquote.com
--goalcast.com
--parade.com
--success.com
--keepinspiring.me
--plantetofsuccess.com
--wisdomquotes.com
--codeofliving.com
--inc.com
--quotir.com
--thoughtco.com
--wow4u.com
--quotemaster.org
--wisesayings.com

1 Merriam-Webster Dictionary.
2 Dad the Family Coach, by Dave Simmons, Victor Books, 978-0896939462, 1991.
3 sermoncentral.com, contributed sermoncentral on Jun 18, 2007.
4 https://high5test.com/parenting-skills/.
5 https://high5test.com/parenting-skills/.
6 https://psychcentral.com/lib/the-5-cs-of-effective-discipline-setting-rules-for-children#1
7 https://www.healthychildren.org/English/family-life/family-dynamics/communication-discipline/Pages/Disciplining-Your-Child.aspx
8 https://www.verywellfamily.com/consequences-punishments-differences-kids-1094787
9 Sermoncentral.com, Contributed by Dr. Fred W. Penney on Aug 20, 2019.
10 https://www.jw.org/en/bible-teachings/questions/honor-your-father-and-mother/.
11 https://www.creativehealthyfamily.com/respect-love-your-parents/.
12 https://www.therebelution.com/blog/2016/02/101-ways-to-love-your-parents/.
13 http://marvinlwilliams.com/21-common-ways-children-dishonor-their-parents/.
14 34 Ways to Respect Your Parents, by Cyril Abello https://inspiringtips.com/ways-to-respect-your-parents/.
15 https://inspiringtips.com/reasons-why-family-is-the-best-thing-in-life/.
16 https://www.whatchristianswanttoknow.com/10-ways-to-honor-your-parents/#ixzz7fLH3tzRF.
17 https://www.familylife.com/articles/topics/life-issues/relationships/honoring-your-parents/how-can-you-honor-parents-when-you-feel-they-dont-deserve-it/.
18 Honor Parents; https://www.familylife.com/podcast/familylife-today/.
19 https://bulletininserts.org/children-obey-your-parents/
20 https://thereachinstitute.org/help-for-families/.
21 https://www.familylives.org.uk/advice/your-family/relationship-advice/top-ten-tips-for-a-happier-family.
22 https://time.com/21296/how-to-have-a-happy-family-7-tips-backed-by-research/.
23 https://high5test.com/parenting-skills/.
24 https://evolvetreatment.com/blog/setting-boundaries-ids/?utm_source=syndication.
25 *How Disciplining Children Creates Happy Childhoods*, Focus On The Family, 4-parenting-styles-and-effective-child-discipline.

Resources and Bibliography

1 HONOR YOUR PARENTS: www.womanofnoblecharacter.com/
www.womanofnoblecharacter.com/honor-your-parents/
www.womanofnoblecharacter.com/home-and-family
www.womanofnoblecharacter.com/forgiveness
www.womanofnoblecharacter.com/healthy-strong-relationships/
www.womanofnoblecharacter.com/paid-bills/

2 Tim Challies – blogger and author
https://www.challies.com/parenting/
https://www.challis.com/children/
https://www.challies.com/articles/5-practical-ways-to-honor-your-parents/

3 Ten Ways to Honor Your Parents, by Chystal McDowell; https://www.whatchristianswanttoknow.com/10-ways-to-honor-your-parents/

4 How to Honor Your Father and Mother; https://www.jw.org/en/bible-teachings/questions/honor-your-father-and-mother/

5 Honor Parents; https://www.familylife.com/podcast/familylife-today/

6 Family Issues; https://www.familylife.com/articles/topics/life-issues/

7 Ways to Honor Families; https://ccy.jfcs.org/5-ways-to-honor-our-families-ancestors-and-communities/

8 How to Honor Elders in the Family; https://www.spiritualityhealth.com/articles/2015/09/14/how-honor-elders-your-family

9 Healthy Marriages; https://thehealthymarriage.org/

10 How to Honor Your Family While Starting Your Own; https://thesharpgentleman.com/how-to-honor-your-family-while-starting-your-own/

11 How to Show Love to Parents; https://seekfive.org/show-love-to-your-parents-2/

12 Ways to Show Love to Parents; https://inspiringtips.com/ways-to-show-love-to-your-parents/

13 Ways to Respect Your Parents; https://inspiringtips.com/ways-to-respect-your-parents/

14 Reasons to Love Your Parents, by Matthew Moody; https://www.therebelution.com/blog/2016/02/101-ways-to-love-your-parents/

15 Duties We Have Toward Parents; https://wwwcreativehealthyfamily.com/10-duties-we-have-towards-our-parents-when-they-get-older/

16 Respect & Love Your Parents; https://www.creativehealthyfamily.com/respect-love-your-parents/

17 Must You Love Your Parents to be a Good Person? https://blogs.webmd.com/relationships/20110504/must-you-love-your-parents-to-be-a-good-person

18 Ways to Love Your Parents While Alive; https://www.thesparkng.com/hub/8-ways-to-love-your-parents-more-while-theyre-still-alive/

19 Parenting; https://www.medicinenet.com/parenting/

20 Parenting With Love & Logic; https://www.medicinenet.com/parenting_with_love_and_logic/views.htm

21 Parenting Principles; https://www.medicinenet.com/parenting_principles_pictures_slideshow/article

22 Raising Children; https://www.parentingforbrain.com/raising-children/

23 How Parents Can Raise a Good Child, by Katherine Lee; https://www.verywellfamily.com/how-to-raise-a-good-child-620110

24 Nine Steps to More Effective Parenting, Reviewed by: Kids Health Medical Experts; https://kidshealth.org/en/parents/nine-steps.html

25 Raising Children, by Ana Nelson, July 27, 2022, https://biblereasons.com/raising-children/

26 Ten healthy discipline strategies that work; https://www.healthychildren.org/English/family-life/family-dynamics/communication-discipline/Pages/Disciplining-Your-Child.aspx
27 The Better Way to Discipline Children, by Claire McCarthy, MD, https://www.health.harvard.edu/blog/the-better-way-to-discipline-children-2019010115578
28 Five Different Types of Child Discipline, by Amy Morin, LCSW; https://www.verywellfamily.com/types-of-child-discipline-1095064
29 Discipline Tips Used By Parents Who Have Well-Behaved Kids, by Jessica Tucker; https://www.msn.com/en-us/lifestyle/parenting/discipline-tips-used-by-parents-who-have-well-behaved-kids/ar-AA11Y0W4
30 How to Disciple Children: Where Do We Start? https://raisingeverydaydisciples.com/discipling-children-where-do-we-start/
31 Kids That Change the World: Disciplining Children at Home; https://growingdawn.com/discipling-children-at-home/
32 How Disciplining Children Creates Happy Childhoods, by RHONDA ROBINSON; https://www.focusonthefamily.com/parenting/how-disciplining-children-creates-happy-childhoods/
33 Twenty One Ways Children Dishonor Their Parents; http://marvinlwilliams.com/21-common-ways-children-dishonor-their-parents/
34 Ways to Respect Your Parents, by Cyril Abello
https://inspiringtips.com/ways-to-respect-your-parents/
https://inspiringtips.com/reasons-why-family-is-the-best-thing-in-life/
35 Reasons Children Need to Obey Their Parents; https://www.challies.com/articles/3-reasons-children-need-to-obey-their-parents/
36 Parental Authority Over Grown Children; https://www.focusonthefamily.com/family-qa/parental-authority-over-a-grown-child/
37 Children, Obey Your Parents; https://bulletininserts.org/children-obey-your-parents/
38 Don I Need to Obey my Parents? https://yuriystasyuk.com/do-i-need-to-obey-my-parents-on-everything/
39 Obedience to Parents Benefits & Importance, https://religioncheck.com/obedience-to-parents-benefits-importance/
40 Five Reasons Kids Disobey, Dr. Ron Allchin, https://biblicalcounselingcenter.org/5-reasons-kids-disobey/
41 Tips for Obeying Your Parents - Obedience is Key to Faithfulness; By Kelli Mahoney, https://www.learnreligions.com/tips-for-obeying-your-parents-712224
42 Top ten tips for a happier family, https://www.familylives.org.uk/advice/your-family/relationship-advice/top-ten-tips-for-a-happier-family
43 How To Have A Happy Family – 7 Tips Backed By Research, By Eric Barker, https://time.com/21296/how-to-have-a-happy-family-7-tips-backed-by-research/
44 Fifteen Secrets of Happy Families, by Denise Mann; https://www.webmd.com/parenting/features/15-secrets-to-have-a-happy-family
45 Ten Habits That Form A Happy Family, by Adam Mann; https://www.lifehack.org/293756/10-habits-that-form-happy-family
46 The Do's and Don'ts of Disciplining Your Child; Jan 29, 2019 in Health Tip of the Week, Contributed by: Jason Lewis, PhD, and Ariana Zahn, MA; https://www.chop.edu/news/health-tip/dos-and-donts-disciplining-your-child

About the Author

The author graduated from the Business School at Indiana University and obtained a master's degree at Georgia State University in Atlanta. His first career was as a senior executive with a top insurance and financial institution, where he spent a number of years directing strategic planning for one of their major divisions.

In the 1990s he founded an online Internet business which he sold in 2010. He began to write and publish books and materials that led to an interest in personal life planning. This resulted in combining the wisdom of wise sayings and proverbs with life planning and the result is the Life Planning Series and the Life Planning Handbook.

The author, his wife, and two of his children and their families live in the Nashville, TN area.

WEBSITE: http://www.lifeplanningtools.com

AMAZON: www.amazon.com/author/jswellman

Contact Us

	www.lifeplanningtools.com info@lifeplanningtools.com	Website Email
Facebook	JSWellman	
	www.amazon.com/author/jswellman	**Author Page**
Life Planning Series	www.amazon.com/dp/B09TH9SYC4	
	www.lifeplanningtools.link/newsletter	**Monthly News Letter**

You can help

IDEAS and SUGGESTIONS: If you have a suggestion to improve this book, please let us know.

Mention our LIFE PLANNING books on your social platforms and recommend them to your family and friends.

Thank you!

Make a Difference

"The law of prosperity is generosity.
If you want more, give more."
Bob Proctor[57]

Have you ever done something just out of kindness or goodwill without wanting or expecting anything in return? I'm going to ask you to do two things just for that reason. The first will be just out of the goodness of your heart and the second to make an impact in someone else's life.

It won't cost you anything and it won't take a lot of time or effort.

This Book

First, what did you think of this book? Give the book an honest review in order for us to compete with the giant publishers. What did you like and how did it impact you? It will only take you several minutes to leave your review at: **https://www.amazon.com/dp/1952359538**

Follow the link above to the Amazon sales page, scroll down about three quarters of the page and click the box that says: "Write a customer review." It does not have to be long or well-written – just tell other readers what you think about the book. Or, just score the book on a scale of 1 – 5 stars (5 is high).

This will help us a great deal and we so appreciate your willingness to help. If you want to tell us something about the book directly, you can email us at: info@lifeplanningtools.com.

Give Books to Students and Employees

Secondly, do you know any schools or organizations that might want to give this book or our Life Planning Handbook to their students or employees?

Here is how you can help. If you send us the contact information and allow us to use your name, we will contact the person or persons you suggest with all the details. Obviously there would be special pricing and if the order is large enough, a message from the organization's CEO could be included on the printed pages.

Alternatively, you can personally give a copy of one of our books to the organization for their consideration. We would recommend our Life Planning Handbook, but some organizations might be interested in a specific subject. If they are interested in this partnership with us, they should contact us directly.

It is not that difficult to help someone live a better life: just a little time and intentionality. Let us hear from you if you want to make a difference in someone's life!

J. S. Wellman
Extra-mile Publishing
steve@lifeplanningtools.com
www.lifeplanningtools.com

Wisdom Without Action is Just information!

Love and family light up the darkness.

Love and family light up the darkness.

Love and family light up the darkness.

www.ingramcontent.com/pod-product-compliance
Lightning Source LLC
Chambersburg PA
CBHW060320050426
42449CB00011B/2573

* 9 7 8 1 9 5 2 3 5 9 5 3 8 *